A Little Bit of Wisdom

Horace Axtell, Nez Perce Elder, photographed at Bear Paw Battlefield, Montana.

A Little Bit of Wisdom

Conversations

with a Nez Perce

Elder

by

HORACE P. AXTELL

and

MARGO ARAGON

A James R. Hepworth Book

CONFLUENCE PRESS
Lewiston, Idaho

FIRST EDITION

The publisher hereby acknowledges the generosity of several individu-
als who helped make the publication of this book possible: Mr. Tim
Crawford, Ms. Kathy Hansen, Mr. William Hewlet, and Ms. Gaetha
Pace. *Muchismas gracias*. The publication of this book is also made possible, in part, by the generosity of The Idaho Commission on the Arts
(a State agency), Lewis-Clark State College, and the Lewis-Clark State
College Foundation.

The cover photograph of Horace Axtell is by Mark E. LaMoreaux, the
frontispiece photograph by Stan Hoggatt. For permission to reproduce
other photographs the authors especially want to thank Michael
Cordell, the staff of Nez Perce National Historical Park (Spalding,
Idaho), and Ben Marra Studios.

Library of Congress Card Number: 96-085612
ISBN: 1-881090-23-X

Published by
Confluence Press
Lewis-Clark State College
500 8th Avenue
Lewiston, Idaho 83501-2698

Printed in the United States of America.

For

my wife, Andrea Axtell, and my children: Charles William Axtell, Purnell G. Axtell, Steven Andrew Axtell, Nellie Jane Axtell, Harlene Kay Kidder, Delores Jean Bohnee, Elizabeth Walker, Brenda Ann Axtell, and Etta Lorraine Axtell

HORACE P. AXTELL

For

my desert family: Raul, Evelyn, Eric y la familia. *And for my constellation: David, Jesse, Cassie, and Zak.*

For all the nimiipu titooqan *who have patiently allowed me to record their words and their lives.*

MARGO ARAGON

Table of Contents

Preface

On most summer weekends throughout the Northwest and Canada, you can usually find a powwow setting up on a reservation. The "doings" attract drummers, dancers, vendors, Indian families, and non-Indian onlookers. Powwows also attract writers, producers, and photographers eager to record the different styles of traditional, fancy, and jingle dances. Elaborate eagle feather bustles fan out from a male dancer's hips, while a young woman's jingle dress reflects the glare of the summer sun on the small, metal cones fashioned from tobacco can lids. The heat and the dust cling to the skin and vex the eyes. The dancing and drumming are usually the first introduction a non-Indian has to Indian culture, but there is much more to Indian people than powwows.

I was making a video documentary about Nez Perce Indian dancers and dances when I first interviewed Horace Axtell in 1992. His dancing combined a style of grace and power that is common of elder traditional dancers. I thought he would be a great person to interview about his personal history of dancing. I was surprised when he told me he had not always danced at powwows.

He said, "I haven't always been this way."

"This way" meant the traditional way, the way of his Nez Perce (*Nimiipu*) ancestors. After my video was completed, I still had many more questions for Horace. He seemed as if he lived in two worlds, one within another. I wanted to know how he was able to do it in a seemingly effortless way. How did he manage to balance the history, culture, and language of one group of people with another? When I asked Horace how he felt about writing a book, he said he would have to give it some thought and let me know.

Probably the last autobiography of a Nimiipu person was published in 1940, *Yellow Wolf: His Own Story*. It is the narrative account of a Nimiipu warrior who survived the 1877 War when the United States Government tried to confine the non-treaty Nez Perce to a reservation. L.V. McWhorter, a Yakima, Washington, rancher and historian, became a lifelong friend of Yellow Wolf's and recorded his story using interpreters who spoke both Nez Perce and English. Since 1940, volumes of books have been written about that war. Chiefs, warriors, women, and children died at the Bear Paw Mountains in Montana as they tried to reach a safe haven in Canada. One chief, Joseph, survived to offer his surrender speech. Part of it was translated "From where the sun now stands I will fight no more forever."

But there is more to the Nimiipu than war. Horace decided the time had come to talk about the wisdom of his elders and his life among them. It is a life that will surprise you. He didn't have long braids until he was in his forties. His first language was *Nimiipuutimpt* (the Nez Perce language) and he was raised a Christian. As a young boy he spent time in *qiwn* (the sweat house) listening to the old warriors who survived the 1877 War. Horace's maternal grandmother knew what the owls meant when they called in the night and what message the Northern Lights sent. His grandaunt was a medicine woman. His great-grandfather fought and died in the battle at the Bear Paw Mountains in the 1877 War.

Horace will say this about himself: "I'm not perfect. I've made some mistakes."

He has earned the grace that comes from a difficult life lived without bitterness. In his unique way he helps people understand that the words, teachings, and practices of his "old people," as he calls them, are still worth listening to today.

Over the course of a year or so, I drove to the home Horace shares with his wife, Andrea, and the children and grandchildren who regularly visit them. I set up my tape recorder and attached a microphone to his T-shirt. He sat in his favorite recliner and stroked the old Siamese cat who liked to perch on his knee. Horace would clear his throat a few times, gently pull on his silver braids of hair, and this is what he said . . .

Margo Aragon
1996

A Little Bit of
Wisdom

In 1885 they gave allotments to adult people so they could go and claim a piece of ground to live on. The people had to have an English name. They didn't know that. They thought you could just go there and tell them who you were and then they would give you the land. It didn't work that way. They had to have an English name.

A lot of them really didn't think about this. My grandfather, on my dad's side, went in there and somebody told him that he should use the name "Stephen." That was his first name, "Stephen."

They asked, "What's your name?"

And he said, "Stephen."

"And your last name?"

So he said, " `*Isluumts*." His Indian name.

"No, that's not going to work. You gotta have a last name. An English name."

So he said, "Well, I gotta go find a name."

He started to leave and this secretary that worked in

Have an Indian Name

the survey office there told him, "Well, here. You can use my last name." Her name was Axtell. That's where we got the name Axtell.

I got letters from this group back east somewhere, that have the Axtell name, inviting me to some of their gatherings, whatever they do. But I wrote back and told them, "I don't know if I would fit into your Axtell society because I am a Nez Perce Indian." So now I don't get any more letters.

I've heard different pronunciations of the word "Nez Perce." The fur traders, Lewis and Clark, or whoever was here, called us Nez Perce (per-say). I think this comes from the French word "nez perce." Most people call us Nez "Pierce." I hear a lot of this and I'm getting to the point now where I like to correct people. And I have—many times.

The last time I was in Washington, DC, I rode in the 1993 Inauguration Parade. The Nez Perce people had a chance to be in the parade. One of our Idaho senators was instrumental in having us come over there and be a part of it. Our new president, Bill Clinton, was being inaugurated. There were a lot of people there and a lot of good feelings. I imagine there were negative feelings also, but that day I couldn't see any of it. Everybody was having good strong feelings. Just about everything that you see in the modern world was there. Everybody felt good. I was there and I felt good.

All the way through the parade the different announcers would always say Nez "Pierce." There was only one guy who said it right. "Nez Perce (purse) Tribe of Idaho." And I wanted to, so badly, go back there and shake that man's hand because he was the only one who said it right. But we weren't allowed to break rank, we had to stay in line. Whoever he was, he made my day.

We always like to say we're Nimiipu, which means "We, the people." As far as being mispronounced, it's not really offensive to us. It's just the knowledge some other people have about the Nez Perce Tribe.

When I was a little kid, all the people called each other by their Indian name most of the time. And they used to call me by mine, `Isluumts.

" `Isluumts, go out and get some water." There was no "Hey, you!" words when I was with my old people.

They'd use my name like that. I was used to that. Seemed strange going to school and hearing this other name, "Horace." But I finally got used to that, too.

As long as we stick to our old Indian traditional ways, there's always that connection.

> You must try to speak your language.
> You must have an Indian name.

Many of these things are happening right now. Our young people are coming out and bringing out these old names and being named. I think this is happiness to the elders of today, to see young people want to be named and have an Indian name. Many of our young people are letting their hair grow and they understand now. Maybe this is because some of us are like that. There must be something that we're doing that our young people are wanting to do now.

And it's good to have an Indian name. You want to hang on to your Indian ways. I got my name on the day I was born: November 7, 1924. Way out in the country, there was nobody else around but my grandaunt. She named me for my grandfather. She named me "Isluumts" and I've had that name all my life. I received my English name for one of my uncles that died. His name was Horace Moody. My name is Horace Percy Axtell. I got the name Percy, my middle name, from a friend of my dad's. He was a postmaster down in Stites, Idaho.

A lot of these Indian names come from relatives. The names stay in the family. It goes down the ladder. Grandfather, grandmother, grand-aunt, aunt, coming down the line. Sometimes a person will give a younger grandchild their name, so there will be two of them for a while. When a person wants to receive a name, especially now, they should go out and ask different people. If they want to choose a certain name, ask if there's anybody who wants to use that name. Maybe there's an older person who wants to keep that name in reserve for one of their own children or their cousins or brothers or close relations. They ask each other if they're going to use that name. If everybody gives the okay, then they go ahead and use it. Otherwise they'll have to search and get another name.

I got into a problem like that one time. During the Name Giving Ceremony I was asked to speak. One family had chosen a name. They chose his name and it came from their direct ancestor. When I got up to get ready to pass that name over to this young man, I asked the people if there was any reason why this young man should not be named that. Nobody responded, so he got to keep the name.

After, this one old lady came up and gave me the devil. She said, "That name was in my family." I explained to her it wasn't me that gave him this name.

I told her, "Well, I'm sorry if I made you angry, but it wasn't me. I asked everybody if this name was already cleared and nobody answered me. So I'll take you over to talk to these people who want that name."

I took her over and while they talked I walked away. I found out later that the name stayed. These people came all the way from San Diego, California, to give that ceremony in Kamiah, Idaho. They had all their things laid out there. She didn't protest or say anything until after they got through giving the things away.

I told her, "They gave their things away. That name's official."

I didn't want to argue with her but she kept wanting to argue with me. She didn't want to argue with the other people, she wanted to argue with me. I listened the best I could. I kept telling her that it wasn't me that done this. I was speaking for the people. I still hope she forgave me.

They always want some elder to get up and speak at a Name Giving. I try to analyze the name. Most of us don't know what they mean anymore. The names are so hard to interpret. Just like my own name. My own name, I don't know what it means. My great-grandfather's name, I don't know what it means either. I just have my own idea, but I don't say, "This is what it means." I just have the feeling, "Maybe this is what it means."

Back then everybody had their own names. And they used their names everyday. It was just this one name. They didn't have a first or second name — or middle name — just one name. Each member of the family had this one name and they could identify with just this one name. Most of the families respected everybody else's names. They honored other Indian family names.

Another thing that made names more valuable was they called each other by relationship or kinship: their father, mother, sisters, uncles, aunts. With the uncles on your father's side, the terms were different than on your mother's side. A woman or girl had different terms for older brother and sister, younger brother and younger sister. The boys had different terms for older sister and older brother and younger brother and younger sister. All different ways to say it. It wasn't all just "sister" or "brother." You could tell a man was talking about his sister from his mother's side or his younger sister or his older sister. You could tell when a man was talking about his uncles on his father's side or on his mother's side. That's the way relationship words are. My daughter's children call me *pilaqa'*. My son's children call me *qalaca'*.

The old belief is to have an Indian name to get to The Good Land, The Good Place. Same way with the war dance, dancing in The Circle. To become active in the

War Dance Circle or Seven Drum Religion, you have to have an Indian name. That's why you see a lot of times, before a pow-wow, a Name Giving Ceremony.

Some words are different between the Up River dialect and Down River dialect. I grew up on the prairie and it was a little different, too. Words and pronunciation are a little bit different. We were known as the Prairie People. They called the Kamiah People, "Up River People." Lower People were referred to as "Down River People." We don't use these words now — they're just places to live.

.

S *trong*
Spiritual

I was baptized in the Christian religion in the old Meadow Creek Presbyterian Indian Church. I believed in Santa Claus just like anybody else. I grew up that way. Our old ministers, before they really became ministers, would preach. Somebody would tell them stories about the Bible and then they'd preach on it. Then it got to the point where some other non-Nez Perce preacher would come and preach. Another man would translate, not-word-for-word, but phrase-for-phrase. It's very hard to interpret English word-for-word according to the Nez Perce language. It comes out backwards.

When Christianity came to our country, it became so strong among the Indian people. When they became Christians, they done away with all their buckskin outfits and feathers. They either gave them away, buried them, burned them, or destroyed them. I think Grandmother buried hers. They were told it was heathen to have all these things. And they done it. They

F e e l i n g s

got rid of them. She kept cornhusk bags and beaded bags, but nothing like a buckskin dress or beaded moccasins.

Also, the men had to cut their braids off. I guess they were supposed to destroy them, too. My granduncle had long braids. When we went to the Presbyterian Church, the other men all had hair cuts. I used to wonder about that. How come some of the men had long hair? I started reading about the missionaries and I found out why. They let the women have long hair. My grandmother had braids and she was a Christian. My grandmother and grandfather became Christians and this was how I was raised. Christianity became so strong. That's the way it was. That's the way my grandmother was. Even though she was a Christian, she remembered a lot about the old ways. They told her it was a sin to go war dance. But going to war dances is part of the Indian way of life. Our way of life was part of this war dancing, part of the stick game, part of the sweat, part of the *weyekin*. They were separate and never mixed them together. She used to talk about the ways of the old people, how they knew things and practiced these things.

On Sunday, the seventh day, we were taught not to play, sweat, or work. It's against this way of life. So a lot of these things went right along with the new religion—Christianity. We were supposed to have everything done by Saturday. That's the day of preparation. The word for Saturday is *halxpawit'asx*. It means "the day before Sunday." And the term for Monday is *halxpaawinaq`it*, the day after Sunday. The word for Sunday is *halxpaawit*. That makes you understand that Sunday is a sacred day.

You never seen them go to watch war dances. You never seen them go watch gambling or stick games. They just stayed away. That was the strength of the religion in them days. The old people used to question one another about watching a war dance. Just to go watch, that was even a no-no. It was a sin. Nowadays, it's a lot different.

I see a lot of people that, I guess you would say, are devoted Christians today. But I still see them at war dances. I even seen a lot of them participate and wearing buckskin, feathers, and dancing. It brings back to mind the old people and how different it is now. I wonder how the old people would take this.

A lot of our old elders, after they became Christian people, had to cut their hair. Now you see young people speaking in the Christian churches and wearing braids. It was not the proper thing to do when I was growing up. It wasn't allowed. Like I always say, "Modern times has made a lot of changes in our rules and our ways." I don't like to say too many things that may hurt or change the feelings of these people, because I can see they're trying. They're trying hard to be complete Indian, complete Nez Perce.

Back when I was young and going to the Christian churches, all the women sat on one side and all the men sat on the other side, just like at the Long House. We still do that in the Long House. We face east and west. I used to see this in all the Christian churches. It's not like that now. Sitting on different sides has a purpose in our Indian religion. It all has a place. It has strength. I don't know the purpose for that in the churches. There's so many things that have changed and been overlooked.

When we bring in the cultures of another tribe and use it in our own, we're mixing it up. If you're a Nez Perce and you're trying to use somebody else's powers or their religion or any other thing that other tribes do, it may be neat. Maybe it looks good—feels good and everything—but that doesn't make them a complete Nez Perce as far as I'm concerned. When I talk about our Nez Perce ways this is what I mean:

No mixture of any kind of the old ways.

We can really understand this about the people in the War of 1877. They were all full-blooded Nez Perces and they were trying to get away so they could be complete like that. They didn't want to take up any of these new things that they were trying to make our people do, as far as Christianity or spirituality goes, or any other thing.

My first experience with the Indian religion was from my granduncle Amos. He was my grandmother's brother. He lived at Culdesac, Idaho. Once in a while I'd stay with him. He had bad legs and was kind of an invalid. Sometimes he could go and get around on crutches, but he also stayed in bed a lot. One day, just him and I was at his house. So he called me over to his bedside and he told me, "Well, I'm gonna get ready." He'd wash his face with soap and water.

Then he'd say, "Get my comb."

I'd get him his comb and he'd comb his hair and braid it all nice looking. His hair was white, about like mine is now on the top. His hair was all like that. And being inside a lot he had light colored skin. He wasn't dark complexioned. He was a tall man, maybe close to six foot. After he'd wash he'd say, "Go get me a dipper full of water." I'd go get him some water and he'd drink water and say, "I will now sing."

He'd sing these Indian religion songs and I'd be so impressed. He could sing pretty good for an old guy. I'd lean against the bed with my arms resting on the edge and listen to these songs. Seems to me like it was doing something, like the songs were going upward. I kept watching him. Each time he'd get to singing songs, his hand would be swinging and keeping rhythm. I never did ask him why he was doing these things.

When I'd go back home I'd think about these things. I'd play out in the woods and I'd get tired and lay down somewhere and take a nap, take a rest. I'd lay there and hear the wind blowing through the trees. It would seem like a song. It was almost like hearing my granduncle singing.

At different times, in different places, I could hear these songs. I could hear him singing. When I was in WWII, I got in some tight spots. Once this man and I were guarding our equipment at an outpost. The two of us were sitting out there watching over it. It was nighttime, so he said, "Well, you go ahead and sleep and I'll watch. When you wake up, then I'll sleep."

We were sitting in the foxhole and I went to sleep. I don't know how long I slept. I don't think it was very long. I could hear my granduncle starting to sing. In my dream I was a little bigger, because the bed was way down. I couldn't rest my arms on the bed, so I stood there and watched him sing. He was singing louder and louder. Now he was really singing loud. Louder and louder. All of a sudden that woke me up. When I woke up I seen my partner. He was sound asleep. I heard noises. I woke him up and said, "Let's get out of here."

We jumped out and rolled down the side. We got out of there just in time, because there was an explosion. After that I was pretty strongly in favor of singing the songs. I was convinced. After all these years, I find there are songs for trickling water, songs for the whirl-wind, songs for the sunrise, and so many others. That's the affect I was getting when I was growing up and I didn't know all this. We lived out in a wooded area, right along the creek. We used to go down there and fish a lot. I could sit along the edge of the creek and hear the water. When you hear the water running a certain way you can almost hear a song. That's the way it affected me.

Now that I'm in the Indian religion, these things are becoming a reality. It's like a miracle. That's what makes me believe in our old people, our elders and ancestors. This religion was here way before it can be recorded. It's that far back. I believe that. My great-grandfather was a warrior and fought for the cause—to take this religion and go somewhere where they could practice it without having to be on a reservation worshipping the Christian way of life. It is great to know our ancestors—our old people, our elders—had set these kinds of guidelines for us to follow because they're still being used and practiced today.

We do what we can in our own way. We still try to carry on with the Indian religion. Long as I can remember, we were looked down upon by people. That's the way it's been. Still, they mingled with us at war dances, powwows. I never keep track, but a lot of Christian people come and ask me if I would, when their time comes, sing for them. I wonder about crossing the old ways and new ways. It causes some confusion to worship in the Christian way and still allow them to go ahead and watch the powwows and participate. Do some of the things, but not all of the things. I don't know. I can see the difference now. Christian men wear long hair. I don't look at it as being critical. It makes me think of the old people. When they got involved with something, they done the best they could. The old people were strong and that's what they did, no matter what it was. They brought it out strong.

In our religion, we have honor and respect for all the other religions. They can come and participate or worship with us, take part in our religion. I don't think nobody ever tries to convert one another to our own way of life. Same way with our religion. We don't go around knocking on doors to try to promote our way, our religion. I think the reason our spirituality is so strong is because it comes from our old people, our old ancestors. They done it in a spiritual way. They respected it. Some of us don't do all these things, but we don't put one another down for this. Some of us are strong believers in our old people's teachings, our old ways. The powers of our people are very strong. The way I feel about it, it's what carried them so far in the wars because they believed in all these things. They used it in the rightful manner. They used it in the way they were taught and told by their elders: do one thing and do it right. Do it in the manner that our old people done it. That's the reason all these things are so strong when you do them.

If you could only have listened to the words of our old elder. He said, "There are many different denominations and religions in the world. And we're a part of that. Respect all the others and, hopefully, they'll respect ours. We do this because our Indian people have always done this.

"The elders taught us the ways, gave us directions. We have to uphold this, because they left this for us. Never let this go. If we let it go, we're disobeying the instructions."

He expressed it so beautiful. It's like a set of rules we all follow. A good illustration of this is the way you track an animal or the way you look on the ground to lead you to where the animal is. This was once told to me by a man.

He said, "This is what we do. We look at these tracks laid by our ancestors and we follow them to where they are now. These tracks lead us to The Good Land, The Good Place, where all Indians go after they have spent their time on this earth."

This is why it is so important to seek the wisdom of these tracks you see—like you imagine tracks on the ground. You follow these and then you look ahead. You look ahead to see far beyond, where they are now. And that's when you prepare yourself to follow the wisdom and the instructions of the old people. Many of the elders that have already gone I knew personally. I can remember some of the ones I knew and this connects me to them. Now, when I need to solve a problem or help someone else solve a problem, it's this wisdom that helps. It's not the wisdom that I have. It's the wisdom that I learned and picked up from following these tracks.

The Seven Drum Religion, we call it *walaḥsat*. It means "Jump up and down." They also used to call it *'ipnucililpt* "Making yourself turn." I think the interpretation is the seven days of the week. They always have a song for each day of the week, seven songs. We always sing in sets of seven. One, two, three sets, or whatever. Some places, like the Nez Perce Long House in Nespelem, Washington, will sing twelve songs. It just depends. I think it's very proper. We don't have set rules or memberships. We don't have roll call like a lot of places, or whatever you have to do to be a part of a church. We don't even pay a membership fee. It's nothing like that. It's all free.

Free means no payment.

We don't even take up a collection or anything, because money is something else. It's necessary for a lot of things, but we hardly ever use that word in our religion. Everything is a gift. I think the word "gift" is a very, very important word. Our children, our food, our daily lives, eyesight, hearing—everything you can think of. Our hair. It just goes on and on. We receive these gifts from the Creator.

In our Long House, everybody knows that when the sacred floor is open, people can go out there and speak. They speak to the Creator from their hearts if they want to pray or sing or dance. There's no guideline there. It's open. It's always encouraged that people go out there to do this.

We don't have no set time to finish. If we need to carry it for a whole morning or afternoon, we do it. There's no time limit. When an Indian speaks there should not be a time limit. A long time ago I used to hear the old people talk and they just talked and talked. Nobody got up and told them to stop. There was respect for the old ways and the old people. On top of this, none of it was written down. It was just taught from one heart to another. I think that's what makes it so strong to me.

So much has also been given to us by our old people. There are some strong spiritual feelings that I gather from being so concentrated on what my elders would do and what they did do. That's the feelings I get from this. I hope I don't hurt anyone by this. I don't think I do. I spoke about this to several people, especially some of my elders, and they thought I had done the right thing. So I feel comfortable with that.

Indians are changing, you know. We're going back to our old, old spirituality. Spirituality among the Indian people is becoming very, very strong. Some of them are a bit mixed. Some of them try a little too hard. The religion of our old people is the religion that was here in this country long before the non-Indian people came. That's not only here in the Nez Perce country, it's all over. Every reservation and tribe has their own spirituality, their own way of communicating with their Creator, their directions, way of life, their culture. It was here.

I see a lot of non-Indian people beginning to understand and they're more interested in what life is. They're starting to connect it with the past. They want to learn more about the history of our people. Not just about the wars we were engaged in. A lot of the books that were written about the Nez Perce are mostly about the wars.

They make us sound like that's all we were—a bunch of people wanting to war all the time. But we weren't. As I understand it now, the War of 1877 was a war to keep our religion. All these chiefs—Lookingglass, White Bird, and all of them that you can name—were connected with the Indian religion. The beliefs were strong, not only in religion, but the powers, the visions.

These were different categories. They were not mixed. We didn't mix our religion with our vision quests or powers that we received from the *weyekin*. We didn't mix our religion with the sweat house or the war dances. Each category was by itself. A lot of the old people could do all these things and be leaders in all of them. That's how it goes. It's very important that we don't mix our way of life with other tribes. I know this is happening because a lot of our people are marrying into other tribes and some of these people are bringing their traditions and their culture into our tribe. It's always been taught to me that when you marry into a tribe you become part of that tribe and you follow their ways. But I can't make a lot of people understand this. That is the way they were in the old days. That's the way I gathered it and that's the way I tell people about it. But maybe they think I'm just bringing these things to my own mind. I've seen it and that's the way I believe it and that's the way I present it. Sometimes I don't go to certain places for different things because they got things all mixed up.

Inside the Long House, we always do everything counterclockwise. Same way with our war dances. We war dance counterclockwise. This is because that's the way Mother Earth turns. Quite a few of our Northwest tribes follow this basic rule. Now other tribes in the Plains and the South go and do things clockwise.

Whatever they do is their way and I respect their way. When I travel and go to some of their gatherings or their ceremonies, they do things clockwise. So to honor and respect each other's ways, we do the same. That's the way it should be. I've seen this happen, some of our people will go somewhere and they will dance in their way and go in the opposite direction. To me, I'd feel out of place if I did that because I'd be on another tribe's place. I would respect their way and do the way they do. That happens here, too. We'll still see other people from the other tribes going the opposite way. I don't know. It's just a matter of choice—what a person feels within himself. If they want to show that they're from another land or another reservation, I guess that's up to them.

When we mix things up, they lose their point. If we mix our different ways of our own Nez Perce life, we're weakening the ways of our old people. They taught us these ways. When we mix them up, we're not listening to the word they laid down for us. That's just the way I feel about these things. If we start trying to show each other "No, this is my way and I want you to do it my way," that's weakening. I wouldn't go and try to force another person to follow my way. To the old people, it was not right to do that. But modern times are making things a little mixed up in all our procedures on our land, our reservation.

We don't mix our *weyekin*—our power—with our religion. We don't mix our medicine dances. We have other things too, like stick game. Serenades. Our feasts. Gatherings. Memorials. Name Givings. First Kill Ceremonies. Marriages. Reentering the dancing circle. There are so many things that all have their place, their time, and all their separate meanings.

I think the non-Indian people sometimes think that all Indians have the same ways, the same language. They think we can understand one another and we can't. Back in the old times we used sign language. Now it's becoming a lost art. I know some of it, but I wish I knew more. That was the universal way of communication among all Indian people, all tribes. I guess the sign language that we use now is English.

The Creator gave us the language. He gave us color of skin. He gave us culture, tradition, and so many other things. The Creator made certain things in certain ways. So I always like to encourage people to hang onto what the Creator made them. This is very valuable. Whatever tribe, race, color, or religion we are, we all have really different things that we do to make us who we are.

The Creator made different lands and different kinds of food for all these places, but He still left us basic things. One thing is water. I don't think there's anything in the world that can live without water. I always think about this when I go through the desert. I see things growing there and somehow they have to have water, but maybe they don't need much. A lot of things in life don't need as much as others to exist. Sometimes you have to sit down and just think about this.

If you really believe in the Creator, really want to understand, the Creator made this whole continent. The whole North American continent was made for us people with darker skin. And this got changed. Still, in my heart, this is the country the Creator made for us. It's still here. It still is our country. I'll always believe that the Creator made it for us. You see so many different things happening now. Mother Earth and the Creator are making a lot of changes: earthquakes, storms, fires-

something has developed. I don't think it's a warning to us. It's a warning to other nationalities trying to change Mother Earth. It's something that wasn't made to be this way. It was given to us to use. Now it's overused. That's just my outlook on this whole situation. That's why I say, "I'm always standing here and looking around, seeing what's happening all around me."

When you get older, you start realizing some things. There's a point where you begin to see all the things happening around you. You start understanding things. You start realizing things happening in the world have a lot of connection with the far beyond, what we call The Good Place. If we do things right, we'll hook up with our ancestors in The Good Place. The only thoughts I have about this is how I changed my religion. I still feel I may see my Christian people. The way I've been told by the elders is that all Indian people go to The Good Place whether they're Christian or in the Indian religion.

Grandmother was the Christian. My grandaunt was a medicine woman. That's where I seen the difference in the two of them. To live among them, they never had any differences. Grandmother would do her prayers in the morning and at night. My grandaunt would sit there. Quiet. If she was doing something, she would put it aside until Grandmother got through. When some of the old people became Christians, they didn't participate in any war dances. They didn't do a lot of things. But some things carried over. The shaking of the hands (handshaking) was always done. The men sat on one side and the women on the other. It was automatic. Some of the songs they used to sing—if you had a drum there, you could beat it and keep time with them. That's the way they sang their songs. They don't do that now. It's a different story.

My grandmother used to sing a translated hymn in the morning. As soon as we all got up, she'd call us downstairs, and she'd have her one song and a prayer. Then we'd go eat breakfast. She'd ask the blessing for the food. At noon she'd ask a blessing. Then at night we'd eat our supper. When she felt like everybody should be getting ready to go to bed, she'd gather us up and sing a song and pray again. Every day was like this. All through my life my grandmother done this. No matter where we were at—in the mountains or camping at the religious camp at Mason Butte. The spirituality is still important to me. Even if you just give a thought. I think about my elders, my ancestors especially. I think about my great-grandfather who's buried in the Bear Paw Mountains. When my thoughts go to the east—my prayers, my songs—I feel like I'm singing to my great-grandfather over there.

I've been asked many times what the distinction is between the leader of the Long House and a medicine man. You have to understand the difference between the medicine man role and the spiritual role. The practices are different. They are not done in the same way. Sometimes one person can be both, but not usually. I don't follow the medicine man role. I gather the Indian medicines that we have, because it was something that was taught to me by my grandmother. Just because of this, some people think I am a medicine man. The role of the medicine man is a lot different than what I do as leader of the Long House. It takes a person with a different aspect on the ways of our people. I don't like to say too much about the medicine man role, because we don't have a medicine man on the reservation now, that I know of.

I guess I could say it this way: there are some people

that try to practice the medicine man role, but I think a person has to be of the Indian way. The ones that I've seen try to practice the medicine man way now are people that don't speak their language. That's not just on our reservation. I've noticed this in different areas where people come and tell me they're a medicine man. I watch them and some of them can't speak their language. To me, that's one of the most important things of being a leader of any kind for the Indian people. The language of the people is the priority of what you should be doing.

I speak the language a lot in the Long House. When we speak to the Creator in our own language and pray to our Creator in our own language, that's where the strength is. I have non-Indian friends come and I try to translate some of the things I say. It has a lot of meaning when you speak your own language at a Nez Perce Long House. When I changed over, there were a lot of things said about me.

That also included the whole Seven Drum Religion, because we used to hear many negative things about us becoming active again. This was from our Indian people. Everybody was saying we were doing things wrong, but what we were doing was learning from other Long House people. They were helping us along and giving us songs to sing. Helping us with all the different activities. They showed us and we accepted it. We done it the way we were taught and told.

Of course, all these criticisms came from the Christian world. Maybe they thought we were stirring up trouble. I don't think we were, but maybe they thought we were. We just done it and kept on doing it. Now we've established ourselves. We don't hear criticism like we did before. Now a lot of the ceremonies that happen on the

reservation, we get asked to do. We're asked to participate because it has to do with the older ways of the Nez
Perce—the cultural, the traditional—everything.

I've had the opportunity to rebury gravesites that
have been dug up. Some were dug up accidently, some
on purpose. Grave robbing. The most important feeling
I have when a person's remains have been dug up is to
get them back in the ground, get them back to Mother
Earth. They've been disturbed and when you disturb
something you feel uneasy until it's all put back. Put
them in the right place, in the right way, and facing the
right direction. To have any bones of our old people in a
museum seems wrong. I don't think they should be
allowed to have them. We've done nine of these reburials now. When we rebury a person's remains, we try to
place the body—the bones and everything—in the right
place and then wrap it, usually in a blanket. All the artifacts and all the things they had, we try to put in a little
bundle with a scarf or handkerchief and place it with the
remains. We sing a song for forgiveness for whyever
this had happened. I think it's proper and necessary to
do these things. We try not to keep them out of their
resting places too long—have them become part of
Mother Earth again.

Some of these were dug up by grave robbers looking
for artifacts. Some of the things that were buried along
with them were very valuable. I was asked by one of the
professors from the University of Idaho what I was
going to do with the artifacts.

I told him, "Well, we got to put them back. Each one
of them was a possession."

I think that's what the grave robber was after. He
got, what I would call, just a little slap on the hand for

doing this. I guess he got fined, but not according to what I would suggest.

This is very, very important: When we give a soul back to Mother Earth, it has more meaning than just placing a body in the ground. We feel this way: all the food, the water, and everything this man, lady, or child consumed has to be put back in the ground. They're being recycled. This is so that Mother Earth will provide them again for someone else, some other place. Even for the unborn. This is why it's important not to disturb these things. I don't think any cemetery should be disturbed.

One time, the City of Asotin, Washington, was digging a pipeline. They were redoing their city water system. They were digging pretty deep and come across some remains. Two of them. So they stopped right there and they called the Tribe. I have to commend these people from Asotin. The Tribe got ahold of me and I took my singers — my Long House people — out there. We placed the remains, buried them, and took care of them in the right way. And the city was so nice about it. It was so beautiful that they felt this way.

During this time while we were doing this, something happened that probably had more meaning to me than anything I've ever done in this manner. While we were singing the songs, I was facing to the east, like I always do. Then I looked over and I seen the ladies looking up in the air. I didn't know until after the ceremony what they were looking at.

They told me four eagles came. Four of them. They circled us three times and then they left. I didn't see them myself. But the feelings I had — I connected it with the Creator who sent these messengers down. This whole thing was not just an act of respect. It was more than that. There's no doubt in my mind that I'm doing the right thing when I have to do these reburials.

As soon as someone died, the older people began to prepare this person for the journey. I will always remember this. They did the complete preparation. They completely bathed the body. They took away the old clothing and sometimes sent it to the Creator by smoke. They burned these personal belongings. This is because they no longer needed these clothes. He's going to wear the clothes in the spirit way when he goes on his journey.

We have a dressing ceremony. The way we dress to go is important. In the Indian religion, I think it's standard that we dress in the way we dressed in the old times—the buckskin clothes, buckskin moccasins, hair wraps, and a special eagle feather. These are the best clothes that our old people ever had. Sometimes the person will gather these things for himself. Like me, I would have my buckskin, my moccasins, everything ready. We prepare. It makes it easier on the family. They don't have to rustle around at the last minute to gather these things up. It's all laid out there, prepared. A lot of people go so far as to pick out their own body handlers. Now that is preparation.

We take the person to the Long House where he or she will spend the last night with the people. We have services, or a wake, all night long. There are other things that happen during this time. The last feast with the person is early in the morning. I don't like to reveal too much because this is very sacred.

One important part of the religion is the way we enter and sit in the Long House while we're worshipping. We come into the Long House from the east side and then we go around to do our greetings. We greet the Long House or the ground—the sacred floor. We greet the people. Then we go and sit down. The women sit on the south side. The men sit on the north side. All our singers and drummers sit on the west side. All the space on the east end is open. This is the way the new day comes to us, from the east. That's where our songs go. Our speeches and prayers all go to the east.

We have many explanations about where we sit. I had one man tell me the women sit on the south side so they can look to the south slopes and pray for all the foods that grow on the south slopes and all the digging and work they have to do. The can also look across to their menfolk and see what kind of clothing and things they could make for them to look nice. The men sit on the north side so they can look for the game and animals and things that have to be done where the trees grow. They too, can look across and see that, maybe, one of their children or family need to have buckskin, so they can prepare themselves to hunt for these certain things. It's a basic procedure that's been with this religion for nobody knows since when. This kind of setup is important during the time a person is going to take the last journey. The people that are up there in The Good Land are waiting in this same manner. As soon as we let him go, he'll have to come in that same way. It's a greeting. He'll have that welcome just like he was entering another big Long House.

We use a wooden box. In time, the box will deteriorate. Long time ago, they just put them in a blanket. The remains become dust again, part of Mother Earth. I think that's the meaning of going back to Mother Earth. But that is our way. Other tribes have their ways. I respect all the ways. I see people putting one another in metal caskets and stone vaults, but that's their way. Our way is so we can become part of Mother Earth again.

We don't believe in cremation, because to give our body back to Mother Earth, so it can turn to dust, is the guideline or tradition. We believe, when you die, your body goes back to Mother Earth and your spirit goes to. The Good Place. As far as I can remember, our Indian people always believed in going back to the Mother.

We don't dig the ground like a day ahead of time of two days or whatever. We dig it that same day the person is going to be put into the ground. We don't, like we say, scar Mother Earth too much or leave her dirt laying outside. We dig the place and soon after we put the body in the ground. Then we put the dirt back in. A lot of us will start after midnight on the day that person is going to be buried. A lot of our people like to be buried at sunrise. Probably the only times we disturb Mother Earth is when we dig our roots or dig our special bathing places or dig our burial place. It's important we have this person in the ground before midday. Everything has to be done before the noon feast.

During this time we're not all sad. Once in a while some things happen and there's laughter. To us, this is a happy time. This person has lived his life and is going to where the most beautiful place in the world is. To us, that's what the understanding is. It's a place where our ancestors are. Our loved ones have already gone and he or she is going to be there with them. This is why we prepare for this important day.

When we come back to the Long House, the people that are left behind, the relations, come in and we'll handshake. They come in and shake hands with all the people that supported them, all the people that witnessed all this. It's very important that they greet these people with a handshake. We have the noon feast, and all the foods are brought on the table and the feast is carried on. The person ate a lot of different kinds of food in his lifetime. A lot of them were probably his favorite foods. To eat all these different foods is like medicine to the family that is left behind. All these things are brought out and we eat together.

Some of the articles, clothing, or possessions of this person that died are distributed or given away to people. It isn't necessary, but to some people it is.

In these modern times, the Christian religion has their own funerals. But there are some Christian people who want to be buried in this Seven Drum way. This has happened to me several times. It's the person's choice how he wants to be buried. It all comes to that same thing we talk about—the preparation. I've been asked a lot of times, way in advance, to help send someone to The Good Land.

They say, "Whenever it becomes my time, I want you to do this for me."

I've been called from different places where I'm attending a conference or doing things as far away as Washington, DC. I've been called and told a certain person has died. Most of the time I know who died. I also know that I got to get back because I made a commitment to that person. It's a great responsibility to be asked and you have to follow through. We pass the word among ourselves and prepare. We don't refuse anyone. I've heard other religions refuse certain people for their lifestyle or whatever has happened. Sometimes they refuse the marriages, too. In our religion we don't refuse anyone. It's up to the Long House to get together and make it the best journey we can for that person.

We don't know where some of our people are buried

along the trail that they followed during the war. To me, this whole Nez Perce Trail has become a sacred place. It has also become a national historic trail where people are going to walk. I hope that's all they do. Just walk along the trail and try not to disturb anything along the way, because as far as I'm concerned, it's sacred ground.

The instructions that the old Chief Joseph gave to his son were: "Don't sell my bones." And he didn't. They were taken away from him. Taken away. If I am buried on some of my land, I hope my children will not sell my bones. I tell my children about it. I think they understand, but then I know they really won't understand, until they get a little older, how these kinds of feelings affect your mind when you become older. This is what's happening to me.

We used to call this one old lady, "Grandma." Everybody called her Grandma. She went to the Long House all the time. She would never miss. The time came when her age was making her become weak and ill and she knew this. When she got confined to her bed she became weaker and weaker. She called her step-daughter in and asked her to call me.

She said, "I want my *miyooxat* to come and sing. There's people looking in at me. People want me to go and I don't want to go yet. I want my *miyooxat* to come and sing songs. I want to rest. These people won't let me rest."

They were spiritual feelings that she had, so I went out there. I sang our religion songs, several songs, and then she started to calm down. After awhile she went to sleep. I closed my singing with the sounds of the bell and when she heard the ringing she didn't really wake up, but she raised her hand. She still had her eyes closed and she raised her hand like we always do when we show the Creator, with our open hand, we have nothing to hide by sending our spiritual feelings to Him up that way. And she did that.

After that she wanted me to come every evening. And I did. She always told her stepdaughter, "Before he goes home, you make him eat."

Then, one day, Grandma went to the Good Place. I had the honor of leading the services. When we were doing the funeral, it made everybody so strong. It was so important to me to do things the way we were taught, to use the proper procedures which I learned from my elders. Even today, I learn from my elders. I still learn. They just put it into your heart and it stays there.

The whole religion is like a preparation. It's a preparation for going to The Good Land or to the place of your ancestors. We all have to go through it. We all know this. In every tribe they have certain ways. Certain guidelines, you might say, have to be followed. That means every day, not just on the seventh day or Sunday. Each day we thank the Creator for this life. On Sunday, we go to the Long House and thank the Creator for this life. We thank the Creator for all the food and all the other things that have happened to us. Sometimes a newborn has come into the family. We also thank the Creator for this.

Each time the sun comes up, it's a new day. We greet these new days with prayer or song. We have special songs for all these things. Very few of our songs have words. The people understand the Indian way of describing songs. A lot of these songs are about nature and a way of life. I learned a lot of songs from a certain person, and at a certain time if I want to sing a certain song, it's like a picture comes to my mind. It just comes out like a program. That's the way I feel about the elder people, and I hope that some of the things that I teach and speak about will be taken the same way. When I pray to my Creator or when I go out to the mountains—listen to the wind, and talk to the spirits—I ask for wisdom.

The non-Indian people were curious about what we did. But now I think the curiosity is being pushed aside and they want to find out the complete nature and meaning of all our traditions and practices. They see things happen at the war dances or other ceremonies. Maybe they think we were doing a show or something, but we weren't. They are important to us. This is part of our way of life and we have special things that we do. We don't just think about them and all of a sudden we'll make up our mind to do it. It all follows procedure. No handbooks or pamphlets are written on this stuff. It's all given from one heart to another, like I've always said. This is the way it's carried out. It's a part of my way of life. I know it was a way of life that my ancestors had. I hope and always pray to the Creator that it will be a way of life for my great-great-great-grandchildren and the people that I know with their great-great-great-grandchildren. We try to encourage all these things to stay alive and stay in the bounds of our people.

I feel like I'm ready. My preparations have carried me to the point where I feel like if I should pass on today, I'll be ready. In my own feelings, my own heart, I feel like I've had a long life. I've completed a lot of things. I'm able to give a lot of thought to many things in my life. I still look forward, too, hoping I can help someone else—share my knowledge, my teaching, and my points of view. Hopefully, it will make some other person a stronger person.

When I was a young boy, we used to listen to an

evangelist on the radio. I can't remember what his name was. My mother liked to listen to the music. Music was always the favorite keeper of her mind. She played piano and sang in the choir. She also listened to Indian music, but back in them times we never had tapes like we use now. I listened to this man preach on the radio. I'd hear him give invitations or ask people to convert. I never gave it too much thought because what my grandmother did was more important to me. It was more important to me to be right there with her. Listening to the radio was something else. I think that whole thing carried over onto television. You see a lot of different evangelists, or what they call these healers, and different people doing things on TV. To me, it's kind of like doing it for the money. It's like a show. You can sit at home and see this show. I sit here and watch football, basketball, and all sports things. Even movies. That's entertainment. It's a different thing to go to a Long House or even a church. You're getting the words from the person that speaks. The vibrations are right there. You pick it up. It doesn't seem right to see it on television. It has a different impact on me to hear someone speak in person.

As a spiritual leader I don't just speak to the people who are spiritual. I go into different places where people are confined. If I'm asked to go to a prison to speak to Indian prisoners, I do that. If I need to speak to somebody in a tavern, I go in there and talk to them. I visit the hospitals. I visit just about every place you can think of. All Indian people are important to me and this is the way it should be. People come to my house and talk to me.

I tell them, "If you need to talk, I have a telephone, but I'd rather talk to you in person."

When we speak to one another we look into one another's eyes and the message goes heart to heart. I think an important part of my belief is to speak to all Indian people. You got to be really open at all times. Some of the things I say, maybe, touches a person's heart. I get calls from New York, Boston, and Oklahoma, telling me this. Even letters. It makes me feel good that somewhere, someplace, I've touched somebody's heart. My wife and I are both on the Council of Elders with the American Indian Students of Science and Engineering Society. This is the importance of spirituality: You're willing to share this with other people and you're willing to counsel at all times. When I'm asked to do invocations, I do it with high honor, because to be asked is important. You stand there and speak for a lot of people. I speak to my Creator in my language for all the people who speak my native language. All the different tribes that I've seen always speak their own language with their Creator. That's the way I understand it and that's the way I practice. It's good to be who you are.

You also got to be able to withstand a lot of criticism. I had a battle with this criticism for a long time, but I think the power of my spirituality has me strong enough to withstand it. I don't get bothered with it anymore like I did when I first became close to my Indian religion. I think the things I do now have brought me close to a lot of people. Maybe not on my own reservation, but in other lands, other reservations.

Grandmother

I was given a little illustration one time. When I was a boy I bent a little tree over and then rode on it. I guess a lot of kids have done that. It was up on our ground, near our house, and it got to be my favorite place. I'd go up there and swing back and forth on this tree. My grandmother, who had a bad back and was humped over all the time, told me this, "You had fun on that tree and it's a living thing. Now that tree is going to be like this forever, unless you pull it back and straighten it up."

I didn't think much of that at first. One day I had a chance to go up there and play on that tree again. I found myself trying to push it back up and straighten it out again. I loved my grandma so much and I didn't like the way her back was. It bothered me, but there was no way we could fix it. But I was there trying to straighten that tree out and I never did do that again. I think Grandma gave me that illustration for that reason.

The only one I ever asked questions to was my grand-

T o l ∂   M e   T h i ∂

mother. I asked her a lot of things. I asked her why my legs would hurt sometimes.

She'd tell me, "You play too hard."

That was true. My legs used to hurt at night. She would take mentholatum or Vick's and rub my legs down and they would cool off. They'd feel pretty good and I'd fall asleep. I had so much confidence in her. She always had an answer.

She had a broom downstairs and she would poke the ceiling whenever she wanted me and Leander, my cousin that was like a brother to me, to do something. She used to wake us up like that in the morning. We had two beds in our room and she'd hit the floor right in between them. You could hear it because it was right by our feet.

One time we were upstairs fooling around and she hit the ceiling with the broom. It got quiet. Then she said, "Old man Arthur is coming with a team and a wagon."

We wanted to see that. He was a blind man. We took

off down the stairway to see. We looked across to the gate and there was nobody there.

She said, "April Fool's."

She really pulled a good one on us. I always remember that April Fool when it comes around. I think about that every year. That's the best one I ever had pulled on me. She had this memory, this mind, to remember a lot of things.

Grandma was always the last one to go to bed. She was the elder and looked after the house to see that everything was in order before she went to bed. I was up in bed one night. We went to bed pretty early in the house at the ranch. We heard the sound of the washstand being used. Then we heard Grandma gagging. She was making all kinds of racket. We all rushed downstairs. It scared us to hear Grandma get sick like that. She had a little flashlight there and she was brushing her teeth.

When she got her breath back she said, "Must be some other kind of toothpaste."

Back in the forties all sorts of things started coming out in these little tubes. She showed us the little tube she was using. It had the color that was for shaving cream. She thought it was toothpaste. Leander was starting to shave. Here was shaving cream she was using for toothpaste.

We thought she would be mad at us, but she laughed. She thought that was pretty funny. She always had an expression, "*Celmon*." I don't know if anybody still uses it. It means "blankness." When the Chinese first come into this area, the Nez Perces didn't know what to call them. The Chinese looked like they didn't have any thoughts or anything, just blank. They rarely smiled or anything. The people used to describe to me how they used to look at them. That's where the expression came in, like when your mind goes blank, you stare and look stupid. No offense to the Chinese people, it's just the way Nez Perces looked at them.

One morning, I was getting ready to go to school and I couldn't find my glasses. We had a little piano and I used to lay stuff there. I looked all over there, and up to my little bedroom upstairs, and all over my things. I couldn't find them. I come back downstairs and looked around again.

Finally, I looked down at Grandma sitting on the floor. She always sewed by the stove, sitting down. She wouldn't say a word, sewing away. She had my glasses on. She didn't want to give them up.

In Nez Perce she said, "You can see good with these glasses."

I told her, "So can I, Grandma. That's why I want them."

She finally gave them to me and I went to school. She used to take my mother's glasses, too. Grandma never did have prescription glasses until later years. An optometrist down here in Lewiston made her a pair. I was there alongside her. I had to translate the letters of the chart. She come through pretty good. He made her glasses and she went down and had them fitted.

When she come out of that place the first thing she did was look all around. She couldn't really straighten herself, because of that back problem, so she had to bend her knees.

"Now I can see really good," she told me. She was proud of them glasses. After that, I never did lose my glasses, either.

When I was about twelve years old, I hurt my right eye. It was in the summer time and a man and his wife came up from Kamiah. He was a pastor of our church, Meadow Creek Church. We used to go to the church on horses. It was four miles on the other side of town where we lived. We'd go Saturday and then stay there overnight. Sunday, after services were over, then we'd go home and get ready for school in the morning.

He had his horses and wagons. My grandmother had her little buggy. Of course, I had to ride my saddle horse. We had to go across Lawyer's Canyon over on the other side, up towards Mason Butte. We call it Talmaks now. We were just getting close to the main road and I was trotting along, galloping here and there with my horse. All of a sudden I found myself on the ground and I was hurt. I knew I was hurt.

A cinch on my saddle broke and I went over sideways. I poked my right eye. I must've landed on the saddle horn or a bag full of rocks that I used for my sling shot. It was bad, because blood spurted all over the ground. Grandmother was pretty scared. She thought I had broken the eyeball.

They had water and they cleaned me up. My mother wanted to turn back and go home, but we were going on this journey and I wanted to go, too. My eye hurt, but I didn't want to say I was hurting, because I wanted to go. I loved that place where we used to go, so we kept on. After we got to that area, my grandmother went and picked some kind of root. She come back and with her little tools she ground up the root and put it in a wet wash rag. She laid it over my eye and just let it soak there. Every once in a while she'd change it.

After we got our tipi set up I laid in there. It was nice. They would go out and pick huckleberries. I laid in the tipi for about three or four days. On the fourth day she took the wash rag off, cleaned it up, and told me,

"Open your eye." I opened my eye and I could see.

"Grandma, I can see you." She was so thrilled that I had my eyesight, so happy. That medicine from Mother Earth fixed it so I could open my eye. Before that, it was stuck shut.

Grandma used to put up two or three tipis in back of the house. They were made out of canvas and tule mats. Each one of these tipis had a purpose. One she would use for drying meat, the other one she used for working her buckskin, and the other one she had for working with her foods. You could always tell when she was going to do a certain thing. Tipi poles are used in a lot of different ways. My grandmother always had poles. Right beside the shed we always had enough poles to make about three tipis. Our house was not very big. If people brought their own tipi, we had the poles. When we went to these old campgrounds, we'd put our poles away and leave them there. You'd see another two or three sets of poles here and there. Nobody would bother each other's—come back the next year and they'd still be there. My mother's poles would still be there. Nobody went and borrowed each other's things. If they did, they put them back. They never, ever stepped on each other's toes. I don't think it's that way anymore.

Some of the things that our old people teach is "think ahead." Waiting for the first roots to come, sometimes Grandma would say, "We can only eat once a day for a while and drink water."

That's the way it was. We always had a way to survive. Always, every year, it was the pattern. Start getting ready. Prepare. She had a lot of wisdom. She also had her favorite places where it seemed like we'd always travel, travel, travel to get to. She'd set up camp and tell us, "Oh, we'll stay here for a few days."

Some of the other ladies that would be there would go out gathering and come back that night. They'd have a whole bunch of berries or a whole bunch of roots. Whatever was there. Everybody had their own special places to dig *qemeś*, medicine roots, gather moss, or fish.

Moss is what we call *hopop*. They're the black things you see on the timber trees. I think Grandma used to get them off of the yellow pine or Ponderosa. She had her special places on the hillside and she knew where there were some places that were easy to get to. She'd make a little hook out of wire and pull the moss down. I had the job of picking it up. Whichever ones she wanted we'd put them in the gunnysacks. We'd take home five or six gunnysacks full. When we come back home they'd bake the *qemeś* and black moss together. After baking they'd grind that up into a cereal with a grinder. Or they'd cut it and chop it into little pieces and then cook it like oatmeal. It becomes black and looks like pudding. Just add a little sugar in there and it's called "licorice soup." I still eat it, but you seldom see it much anymore.

I don't think anybody has ever written down any of these things. Indians, old people, teach and pass them on to the next generation. This is the first time I've ever recorded this, or even spoken about it. I know there will probably be a lot of people saying, "Why is he telling all this?" People should know the old ways our people had. Things are changing so much now. It's becoming a lot different.

During the season when the *qaws* would be plentiful, up around Cottonwood, Idaho and the Camas Prairie, a lot of ladies would come up and see us with their wagons and horses. They'd go digging and peel their roots. They had places where they dried their roots. They'd spend the whole time there until the process was all finished. Then they'd sack them up in these cornhusk bags and leave. Grandma would have a whole bunch of cornhusk bags stacked away. That's when I used to see these cornhusk bags filled with roots. I don't ever see these kinds of bags used like this anymore.

After a wheat harvest, Grandmother and some other ladies would go out into the fields. A long time ago, farmers used to harvest with the old stationary threshing machines. They'd go out in a field and cut the wheat. Then, with a binder, they'd bind the stalks into bundles of grain. When the harvester came, the wagons would go out and pitch all these bundles onto the wagons, haul it, and feed it to the machines. They'd blow out all the chaff and straw into big piles. Some of the wheat the machines didn't quite get.

My grandmother and another lady would take a big canvas and throw a bunch of that straw on it. They'd get on each side and shake it up and down. The wind blows a lot on the prairie and when it got good and windy they'd shake the straw up high. They'd throw that straw up and down like that and the wind would blow the straw and chaff away. After they got all finished they'd shake the wheat out. They used to have things to cover their eyes so they wouldn't get any straw in them.

Grandmother would bring the wheat home, take it out to a flat rock, and build a basket around it. Then she had some stakes made out of willows to hold down the basket. She'd grind the wheat with a little stone hand tool. She'd have enough to make bread or sometimes we ate the wheat for cereal. Of course, wheat was different a long time ago. It wasn't all treated with chemicals like it is now. That was just good, plain, clean wheat. We ate a lot of that.

That's why I think Indian people didn't have that hard a time during the Depression because they knew how to get food and take care of themselves. We used our buffalo hides for different things. We had seven or eight buffalo hides and used them like covers during the winter. We also had some laying on the floor for rugs. Sitting on them, close to the stove, they were warm. That was my experience with the hard time of the Depression. It was hard times, but it wasn't really hard times for us. It was our old way of life to know how to survive.

Grandma told me about some of the hard times, only the winters would last a lot longer than they do now. The old-time winters used to last until sometime in March. They'd start running low on dried meat, all the roots, and things got pretty scarce, so they found out a way to catch fish.

Grandmother and my grandaunt were telling me that instead of ice fishing like they do now, they'd go to a frozen creek, chip the ice around a section, and make like one iceberg. They'd put little holes here and there and a bunch of them would get on the ice and dance up and down. They'd get a good rhythm going and pretty soon the fish would come through them little holes.

I used to wonder about that. I thought, well, she was pulling my leg. But I've had other people tell me this. I guess it's that pressure. The fish would jump and come out of these holes, then they'd go pick them up. That's one of the ways they'd get something to eat, even if it was cold. She told me how our old people crossed a frozen river. They'd use small tipi poles. If you fell through, you could save yourself. It was common sense.

As soon as the weather would start warming, the creeks would start flowing really high and people gathered along the river to catch suckers. They're always the first fish to come up the river in the spring. Grandma prepared a lot of suckers. They're good to eat.

The butcher shop where my grandmother used to trade a lot was in Cottonwood. Every so often she'd get a card in the mail telling her to come on over. They had a special cow that they had butchered with plenty of intestines and other parts of the animal. She was such a special person to them that they would clean it for her. It's a lot of work to clean intestines. She showed them how to do it. They'd run all these garden hoses through and really do a good job.

She'd take the intestines, cut them in sections about a foot and a half or two feet long, and hang them over poles inside one of her tipis. There were special racks that she made for drying meat and things in the tipi. On the ground you could build a fire if you wanted it. After the intestines were dried she'd put them away. When she needed them she'd cut them into little chunks about an inch and a half long and add seasoned corn, garbanzo beans, or any other special food—makes it taste a lot better. It has a pretty fatty taste. I had some here about a week ago. Some people brought some of that over. It felt really good to eat some of that again. We call that *mymy* in Nez Perce. We call weiners and bologna the same thing. *Mymy*. We also ate the *qopas*. I don't know what you call it in English. It's part of the insides. She never did dry those. I imagine now, in the freezer, they can keep a little bit longer.

The butcher shop used to save all these scrap bones for her, too. I'd bring them home and break them apart so that the marrow inside could be seen. Then she'd boil and cook them. She had a special stick and she'd pull out all that marrow stuff and cook that. She'd make a big pot of that and add macaroni to it. I imagine it had a lot of fat in it, but it was good. We ate a lot of things like that when I was growing up. It feels really good to be able to eat some of those things now.

Grandma used to also get kidneys, liver, and heart. She'd always get a hunger for these things. Today, we never get a chance to eat any of that unless somebody old and traditional will make some of these things and bring them to a feast at the Long House or a special dinner. She had a big, old copper kettle, maybe twenty gallons. It was a big size and had a handle and hook on it. She would build a tripod of wood and fire beneath it. That's where she used to boil a lot of these things. She'd boil a whole bunch of stuff together like all them bones and things. It was my job to keep that fire going, but not too big a fire.

"Don't build it too big. It's got to be just right," she'd say.

You got to be patient with a lot of the old people when they do things. Everything's got to be a certain way. I know sometimes now, as I get older, I tell my young people to do something and they're always in a hurry. Always ready to get it over with. Sometimes I got to do it over myself. I always like to do things the way Grandma did it. She took her time, made sure everything was proper. It always seemed like it would fall into place. It was just like clockwork, that whole cycle of conserving. Just about everything had a use. She never got anything at a yard sale.

She was the one person that gave us provisions during the hard times like the Depression years. It wasn't really hard on her because she already knew how to do all this. That's the way they lived a long time ago. They gathered roots, berries, all kinds of fruits, and dried a lot of things. She always had that ability to prepare for winter because that's the way our old people survived years back. They migrated from wherever their winter camp was up to their summer camp. It was a cycle from one place to another as the different foods came into season. In the fall time, they returned to stay close to the rivers where it was warmer.

A lot of the times during the Depression, it got to the point where our shoes were so badly worn that we wore moccasins to school. Even some of my neighbors who were Germans wore moccasins. Grandma made moccasins for them. Our neighbor, who lives in Washington, DC, now remembers that. He happened to visit with me not too long ago. He talked about the time they used to go barefoot. It was a big family—ten kids. They would come to our house barefoot and my grandmother would feel sorry for them, so she made moccasins for them. He remembers grandmother. He said he thinks about her quite a lot.

Borrowed Language

I've heard people say things about the Indian way of life. They ask, "Why do you have to hang on to this?" Always my answer is, "Because we're Indian people."

I'll say, "What nationality are you?" And they'll tell me.

Then I'll say, "Well, can you speak your language?"
They'll say, "No."

I'll say, "Well, did your ancestors, your grandpa or grandma, speak the language?"

"Yes, but my grandma was a Swede" or whatever. "And my dad was Italian."

So there they are. It's good to learn this English language. We call it "The Borrowed Language." But for a lot of the non-Indian people, that's all they know. I had a good friend who worked at the sawmill with me. He was of Mexican descent. A lot of laborers, Mexican nationals, used to come over to this area and work in the peas. My friend said he got pretty embarrassed one time when they come up and asked him to be an interpreter for these people.

He said, "I was so embarrassed. I can't speak my language. All these people are my people and I should have been there to help them, but I couldn't. I really feel bad."

Up on the prairie we had neighbors, and I was picking up a little English. On the first day of school Mom said, "You're going to school today. School starts today."

I really didn't want to go, but I seen other kids I knew going to school. They come back with colored papers and things, so I thought it might be a good idea. I didn't want to go, but I was curious. When I went to school I met the teacher. He was a male teacher and looked awful tough to me. I was kind of scared of him. The first time he raised his voice it scared me because I wasn't used to people like that. At home, everybody talked normal—nobody shouted or hollered, or anything. I would very seldom hear anybody raise their voice. Later I found out he talked so loud because he wanted everybody to hear what he was saying.

I had to learn a lot of things. Things like asking to go to the bathroom or get a drink of water. I always watched to see what the other kids were doing. The teacher never told me about all these things like raise your hand and show two fingers for a drink of water or one finger to go to the bathroom. One time I had to go to the bathroom and I raised my hand.

He said, "Yeah."

I got to go to the bathroom. I seen another guy raise two fingers and he went out, got a drink, and came back. I learned how to do that.

It took me a long time to be able to go and ask questions, because our older people very seldom make you ask questions. When they talk to you, they give you advice. When you talk to younger people, you give them advice and teach them what you want them to learn. It's coming from the heart. That's just the way it was.

It didn't take me long to catch on. I was doing pretty well after the first year of school. My mother could talk English, but she hardly ever did. Everybody talked Indian all the time. Grandmother couldn't speak English. To honor her, we all spoke our language.

This is another thing that brings me back to our language. After I learned to speak English I used to translate for my grandmother. She wasn't able to speak or write English. I was a small child—maybe third grade or a little older. We'd go to the bank, the grocery store, anyplace. I could speak two languages and these people that were doing business with her were starting to be careful because I could speak them right. Sometimes she would refuse. She'd shake her head and say, "No."

Or she would say, "Maybe they should give me more."

And I'd translate, "This is what she says. Otherwise she won't accept." So they would think about it a little more and then change their minds. They would give her more of what she was asking for, like on a lease. And this has made negotiating leases and things a lot easier for me because I have the nerve to ask for more. When I got older, I used to have to witness her signature. Before, she would use a thumbprint for her signature or sometimes an "X." We don't see these things anymore. I tell our young people stories like this and they can't believe it—but it's true.

A lot of the elders, like myself and others, still speak the language. We speak it a lot. The ones that follow the traditional ways—the Indian way of life—always connect themselves to our language. Many of the supposed leaders in our tribe can't really speak the language. I think this weakens their dedication to the people. A long time ago, in the General Council of our tribe, everything was done in the Nez Perce language. Everybody could understand. Everybody knew what everybody was talking about. Modern times has taken this away. A lot of the English language that people talk now is way over the heads of some of the people. Like myself, I'm not a highly educated person and some of the things that I hear I don't understand. And I know I'm not the only one like that. But if they could come out and explain some of these things in Nez Perce, I could grab it like that, because I understand and speak my language. This is valuable because I am a real Nez Perce Indian.

These

Old

Powers

Grandma used to like to talk about the animals. One of her pet things was listening to the animals. We'd be playing outside and she'd holler at us to come in the house. She wouldn't allow us to play in the dark.

"It's getting dark now. Come in. You have to come in."

So I'd come in and tell her, "The owls are talking. I heard the owl."

She'd say, "How did it sound?"

And I'd have to mock that owl. I got to where I'd listen and I'd mock that owl just as close as I could to the way it was making its hoots.

Then she would say, "Do it again." And I'd repeat it again.

"Aaooh," she'd go. "The weather's going to get colder. Bring in lots of wood."

I'd bring in lots of wood. The next morning, boy, it was cold. She knew all that. Same way with the coyotes. I'd hear the coyotes down the canyon and I'd mock those.

"Aaah, I wonder if somebody died."

Sure enough, a day or so later somebody'd come and tell us, "So and so passed on."

Grandma was a Christian woman, but some of those old powers were still there. You couldn't take all that away from her. It was still all there yet.

We used to have a lot of meadowlarks around. We'd hear them flying by in the spring time.

She'd say, "Oh, pretty soon there'll be flowers. Flowers are going to come out."

I'd be coming back from school and along the road would be a big snowbank, but right beside would be this buttercup. I'd dig it out and take it to Grandma.

"See, I told you," she'd say.

They used to call them buttercups "coyote's eyes." That's what the Indians call the buttercup. I remember always digging one of them out and taking it to Grandma, the first one I ever seen in the spring.

Sometimes we'd be riding horses or buggies going to town or to church and we'd see these whirlwinds. Grandma would look at it sideways. Pretty soon she'd look at it again, and if it stayed a long time it meant something, but if it just went on a little bit and disappeared, it was nothing. Once in a while the whirlwind would gather up a lot of dust in the bottom part of it and it would seem like it stopped, but you could see the rest of it rise up into the air. She used to say that was going to be a storm or something to do with the rain. She was always good at predicting the weather. If she saw a lot of cobwebs, especially in the little clods of dirt in the plowed ground, she'd tell us we were going to have a cold weather. And we did.

My grandaunt was a medicine woman. I was told a story about her. A couple years ago my son had a car that broke down over at Pendleton, Oregon. He managed to get it over to his uncle's place and left it there. When he got back to Lewiston he said, "Dad, will you help me go get my car?"

We went over there and it took one whole day. While my son was hooking the tow bar onto the car, his uncle came out of the house. He wasn't feeling very well. He started talking to me in Nez Perce. He told me things about the place there and how he hadn't been feeling too well. Then he drifted into things like medicine.

He said, "This old house is a pretty strong old house. We had medicine dances here."

I told him, "My grandaunt was a medicine woman." His face lit up.

"I got one to tell you about your grandaunt. When I was about twelve years old, my eyes was getting blind.

They took me to her to see what was wrong. She worked on me."

Wherever the pain or the cause is, medicine people will go all over the body until they find it. She worked on him and said, "I think I found it." Since he and his relations had traveled to see her, she stopped working on him to have them eat. She asked him some ordinary questions about the activities he liked to play. Got him relaxed, I guess. He was all worried about himself. She got his mind at ease just by talking to him.

He said, "After we ate we went back and sit on the floor."

The bed was on the floor and she laid a blanket down for him. She sat in the same place again and worked her hands from his neck down. She kept doing that until she got to his legs.

"Got down to the end of my feet and pulled. I could feel something. It felt like something was pulled right out of my body. Whatever it was, she threw it away. She told me to lay there. It was getting pretty close to evening. It got dark and I slept in the corner.

"When I woke up I could see the light. I could see. I can still see. Something had blocked the nerve or something. You can't tell me anything about your grandaunt."

This is the story he told me himself. It sounds unbelievable, but the powers of our old people were natural to them. It wasn't something that nobody inherited. I think about the old warriors and the old people. The *weyekin*—the powers that they got from the animals—gave me another reason not to just go and kill animals for no reason at all. You might be killing somebody's power.

For example, I've had many opportunities to shoot a

bear. I never have shot a bear, because a lot of our Indian names are connected to the bear and the eagle. One time I come face to face with a bear—not a big one, a young one. It was about a year old. I come around a curve and there he was, on the road. I went over to where he was and he climbed a tree. He climbed up about seven or eight feet and peeked around. It was just fun to stand there. I talked to him in Nez Perce.

"What are you doing there? Playing?"

Seemed like he understood. No noise, just playing.

Another time I was fishing way up towards Montana. The creek was way below the road. I had to wade down that creek. It was awful brushy alongside the creek. I had my fishing pole, my bag, and my .22 pistol. Started fishing when I got clear down to the bottom and got everything rigged out. Talk about catching some nice fish. The first one I caught was a cutthroat, about a foot long. I was looking at it and thinking, "Oh, boy."

I waded on down the creek because of the brush on each side. It was slick going. I waded some more, found a good place, and started catching some more fish. I spread my legs apart a little bit because I didn't want to fall. I was taking my time, going slowly.

All of a sudden I seen something, *wheet*, between my legs. It was fast.

"Boy, what was that?"

It startled me a little bit. I looked upstream and, *booh*, it went back down the other way. The next time I waited. Wheet, it come right through my legs again. I turned around, went up the stream a little ways and got out of the water. It was one of them otters. That's when I found out they like to play. I'd move a little bit to one way and sometimes he'd come by my left side or my right side. Boy, they can really move fast, just like a streak. He'd move away from me, then look up at me. I guess we played there for quite a while. A lot of names are connected to the different animals, different wildlife. Also, different things of nature, like the thunder and the rain. All this has meaning.

In 1941, things were happening in countries. Wars were happening. I remember this day especially. It was Sunday, and always some of the people from the prairie would come to our house or we'd go to somebody else's house. We happened to be at our place that day. It was a nice December day. After dinner we were outside playing marbles. Right by our window we had a radio. My mother was listening to Sunday music. I was playing outside with my men and boy relatives. All of a sudden we heard this news bulletin about Pearl Harbor. We all stopped. The Japanese had struck Pearl Harbor. We all went inside and turned the radio off.

Not too long before that day we saw the Northern Lights. They were really bright. Bright lights across the sky. Everybody went out to see them. Someone left the door open. It was cold in the house. Grandma came out with her cane to see what was going on. She looked up and seen the lights. We were all gathered out in the front yard. She came out and stood by us.

She told us, "Long time ago when they seen them lights like that, it's a sign of war."

So when we went back in the house that December day, that's what she was talking about.

"War is coming."

That was the power of the old people. So when we told her about the news, right away she knew our men were going to be gone—going to the war. Grandma gathered roots and dried things. She knew. There was food rationing, gas rationing. When hard times came, we were ready.

This old man we used to sweat with said, "Only things that will scare you, or give you a feeling that somebody or something's trying to scare you, are the live things."

Any of your relations or anybody, I don't see how they could come back and haunt you. I don't believe it. People can do things to you, like what we call bad medicine. They can give you sickness. They can get jealous of you for some reason and use their power—powers we receive from animals or things. They can use that to disrupt your life, make it hard on you. That's the thing you got to watch out for.

That's why they say, "When you show people you're brave, they won't even try to do things like that to you."

They know you're not running scared of them. He told us that. I still believe that way. I've gone to some places where people say they hear things. They're scared. I've been to cemeteries at night and I've never heard things. Several times I've forgotten something there. I just go back and get it, even if it's dark. I don't get scared. I still do a lot of work in the cemeteries. I always think about this old man in places like that.

He said, "Those people there are sleeping. They're resting. They won't bother you."

He made us believe that. I believe that today. The live ones will hurt you. The live ones will wish you bad luck. This is the thing I learned from him.

All My
Uncles

I've learned from my elders to show respect, honor, and love. I had a demonstration by one of my uncles about teasing. One day he teased me and it made me a little angry. So then he told me this.

He said, "Nephew, I tease you because I love you. Because you mean a lot to me. The reason I tease you is because I want you to be able to take this kind of teasing. Throughout your life you're going to be teased in many different ways. You'll be teased by wrongdoings. Maybe you'll be teased by women. Maybe by different things that will make you angry.

"I made you angry. Now you've got to make yourself strong so you can take all this. Because it's just like a trial—a test—to see how you can withstand all these things that nag at you. In time, so much is going to happen to you. You're just a little boy."

But I found out you can take a lot. There, for a long stretch, I forgot this teaching. Some things used to happen to me before I got myself together. I could fly off the handle. Some things would tease me and I was ready to settle it in a physical way—what you'd call fighting. I've got into some good ones because of that. I was one of those people that very seldom backed down from anything. Maybe I'm still like that, but I do it in a different way now.

I tease my people. I tease my grandchildren and my great-grandchildren. I tease them because I love them. Right up to today I get confronted by a lot of things that tease me. But I remember the words of my uncle and it makes me stronger. This is one of the things I want my people to remember me for. But maybe they remember the times when I was a different person. I was quick to make judgments. Jump right to it. When you have to fight for things in life, you become a bit too strong that way. You start hurting people and it's not the right thing to do.

You got to discipline yourself. This is one of the things I hope my young people will run through their minds: the discipline of your own self. You've got to make sure you do the things that are right. That's the most important thing. I had to discipline myself. Nobody else could do it for me. When I was put in prison, other people were out having fun and here I was paying for my wrongdoings. I tell my children about this and I talk about it to my ones that are not really following the right direction.

I warn them, "You could land in a place like that and you won't be free for a long period of time."

I hope they remember this and pass it on to their young ones. Wrongdoing is easy to come by and hard to forget.

When I was young, my uncles taught me how to defend myself. I used to have some little old boxing gloves that my uncles got somewhere just for me.

They said, "You're not a big boy. You're not going to be a very big boy. There will probably be people going to pick on you."

They'd tell me these things: "You're going to have to learn how to handle yourself. Defend yourself."

They'd kinda slap me around and I used to have to swing back at them. They told me to "hit us as hard as you want to." I hit them as hard as I could. They laughed about it. That's how I learned.

I got to box in high school. Never had football games. Our high school couldn't afford the equipment. Some of the skills there taught me you can't telegraph your punches. You got to snap them out there real quick. This helps a lot. After the students seen me box with other students, they didn't bother me.

And then baseball came along. I used to play it all the

time, all day long. My uncles gave me an old glove they had. Back in the forties, the baseball glove wasn't like it is now. Alvin was the one that used to make us have batting practice. He was always so interested in teaching us how to play, how to throw. He'd take a baseball cover and cut part of the seam off and take the hard ball out and then make a ball out of deer hair. My grandmother had a lot of deer hair, piles of it. He'd put some of that in there and wrap it up with tape and make a ball. It was awful light. You could really throw curves with that.

We used to make a practice bat, too. Instead of a regular bat he'd make us use a broom handle and try to hit that ball with that skinny handle. We got to where we could hit it. He could really throw a curve. He'd throw a hard ball. It'd go all different directions and we would try to hit it. Then we'd get into a real game. No problem to hit that ball.

One day, before I got in high school, my uncles were outside sitting around playing cards or something and this one man, who was like an uncle, told me, "Go down and see if Grandma will let us use the car. I want to go to town. I have a letter there." He was from Lapwai and had stayed with us for three years.

We had managed to buy a little car, a '33 Ford, and I started learning to drive. It made so many things easier. I said, "Okay," and I went down and asked Grandma.

She said, "Yeah, go ahead."

We got in the car, just him and I. We drove to town and he got his mail. I guess he had some money in there. Across the street from the post office was a pool hall. We went in there and he got me a bottle of pop. I was sitting there drinking my pop. He was talking to somebody and then they went outside. He was gone for a long time. I kept wondering and wondering where he was. Finally I went out back to look for him and here he was drinking. He was starting to get drunk. He was out there for a long time.

We ran into another uncle there and they both started drinking. I told him, "We better get back home." I was just about ready to drive the car home, but I wasn't a good driver yet. They decided they wanted to go to Kamiah.

I thought, "Oh, we better not take this car. It's Grandma's car." I couldn't argue. They were older than me. We headed for Kamiah.

They decided that I should drive, because they were pretty drunk. So I drove and I drove slow. Back in the old times, car headlights weren't really good. All of a sudden we were going down this steep grade, before you get to Kamiah—it's a long ways down. I took a wrong turn and I don't know what happened. I felt the wheel turn. I was knocked out. When I came to I was thinking, "Sure looks bad."

My boots were torn off. One of my legs was hurting. I could hear somebody moaning not too far from me. It was my other uncle. I knew what had happened, but he didn't. I managed to get him up to the road and I hollered and hollered for my uncle. I guess he got hung up and went clear down to the bottom of the canyon. He must've got hung up on that gear shift knob or something. I know we hit a guard post. I could see that in front of me.

We sat up on that road for a while and a car came. We flagged it down. It was a state patrol. I told them my uncle was way down at the bottom. Instead of bringing my uncle up the hill, they found another way from off the side to get him out. It took a while to get

him out.   They took him to the Cottonwood Hospital.
He wasn't dead yet. Before he died, he told the police-
man that he was driving. I was scared, because I was
driving. I was just fourteen and had no driver's license.
There was no investigation or anything. I could have
been charged with manslaughter or involuntary
manslaughter. That could have happened to me,
because I experienced it from the laws. The officers
took us to the Kamiah Police Station. That was the only
place they could take us where they had a bed. The doctor treated us right there. I had a scrape on my arm. I
guess the doctor was all excited when he poured the
iodine on. Straight iodine. He gave me a burn and I
have that scar yet. We stayed there all night. The next
morning another uncle come and got us. Sad time for
us. I was his favorite nephew and he loved me so much.
I learned a lot from him. It took a long time before I
drove a car again.

Fifteen or sixteen years ago I found out that he had
been hiding out with us. He had done something wrong.
He had caused somebody to have an accident. There
had been a trial or something and he was hiding out. I
get to thinking about it. If I had been older I could've
got in that car and driven it home. I loved him so much.
I guess sometimes you got to disagree with your elders.
He was drunk. When you respect someone so much
that when they're not in their right mind you still respect
them because they're older. We must also show respect
by protecting them from danger, even if they are intoxi-
cated.

The Old Man

Ever since I grew up using the sweat house I was always told that he is The Old Man. We call him *qiwn*, which means Old Man. The name for the sweat house is *wisti-tamo*. He was the wisest, most knowledgeable, strongest medicine man. He was the healer of broken hearts, aches and pains, and many things. We always referred to him as The Old Man — Wise Old Man. People use the sweat house for preparing to go hunt, go fishing, play stick game, preparing to do most anything. I learned so much in the sweat house. I was very small when I remember first going into the sweat house. I just barely remember sweating with my grandmother and mother. The things I learned right from the start is keep your eyes closed, wait for the elder man or elder lady to take care of the water, and listen to what they're talking about.

The Old Man was there all the time. Even when you left to go on a trip, he stayed home and took care of everything. He took care of your home, your sweat house, and watched over them. When we'd go on a journey, the first thing we'd do was go visit The Old Man at the sweat house. We'd be happy to get back to The Old Man. He was there all the time.

Now this is what I learned from being at the sweat house. We'd go there to see The Old Man to get wisdom. Whenever elders sweat, and whoever they sweat with, they tell the stories. They talk about their experiences. They give you advice. They teach you words. Anything. That's just the way it was in Nez Perce ways.

Never, ever in my life did I hear people mixing this with religion. I never heard prayers to the Creator in there. I never heard songs sung to the Creator in there. We were there for The Old Man, The One Who Was Wise. We were there to be with him, to get wisdom from him.

Same way with the women preparing themselves to go berry picking or dig roots, or cut up fish and meat, they got wisdom from The Old Man. To them he was The Old Man, too. There's nothing there about The Old Woman. This is what I learned: Never take away from The Old Man by overruling or overstepping him and start praying to the Creator up above, because you're inside this dome, a round place. It's dark in there. You're sitting in there with no clothes on, bare to The Old Man.

The difference between the Long House and the sweat house is when we sing songs to the Creator to worship Him, we put on our best clothes. We put on our moccasins, our buckskin, fix our hair, and dress properly. That's the only way I've ever learned. Inside the sweat house we can't do that. It's dark in there and you don't have clothes on. But now it's a lot different. I've sweat different places and new people—young people—they're mixing all these things up. Singing worship songs in the sweat house, war dance songs. Some of them pray. It's so different. Many different tribes have different ways. Some tribes do their rituals in the sweat house, sing songs, and they smoke pipes. They do a lot of things. For us, it wasn't this way. I am a Nez Perce and our way has a lot of power and meaning, also. I still like to go sweat in my own way. Clean my body and get rid of some ailment or think about passing some of my knowledge to my children, grandchildren, and great-grandchildren.

There are a lot of little instructions. Some of them are humorous. Bringing the ways of the other tribes into our way of life doesn't set well with some of the elders. One man who told me never to sweat on Sunday said in a joking way, "Don't sweat on Sunday. If you sweat on Sunday you'll go to Heaven like that—naked. You can't go to Heaven naked."

Another man said, "Well, that's the way we come into the world."

"Yeah but," he said, "you're supposed to dress in white buckskin when you go. That's the way you dress when you're buried."

Sometimes people would bring their elders and sweat with them. I seen a young man, and must have been his granduncle, come up and sweat. This young man was going to be married. They only stayed for three days. They were in a hurry.

I must have been in grade school when I helped my stepdad build a sweat house. We tore down the old one and built another one. I helped him do that, so I've had experience on how to build a sweat house. We started from scratch. We went down and whittled on the willows, sharpened the ends, and brought them home. These ends are the big parts of the willows. You take a crowbar and make holes where you want them. Then you line them all up in a circle and poke them all in the ground.

My stepdad would push one over to me and take the opposite one and put it over. They come together in the center of the circle.

He'd say, "Stand right here." I'd stand right there in the center and he'd measure from my chest or whatever height he wanted down to the ground. Then we'd tie the two willows together.

"Okay, get that one there." Then I'd get the willow on the other side. We'd do the same thing to these willows except we'd tie them a little bit lower. We went all around until we got it perfectly even. That's the way he done it. Now everybody doesn't do it that way. I was there to help. That was my job. I got the canvas and covered it up. He made his a lot different than a lot of people do. He'd use gunnysacks on the inside and cover the sweat house in canvas. He'd take dirt and sod and base it around the bottom and just keep building it up.

He built the door frame so it could hold sod. Instead of using all canvas, he'd cover it completely with dirt and sod. It was a hot sweat house. I mean, it was airtight. Our sweat house was about a quarter mile from the house. Our house sat in the meadow, in a high place in the meadow. It was meadow all around. Up at the end of the meadow was a creek. We had our sweat house out there at the edge of a wooded area. We always had plenty of wood for the sweat. A little stream come down through there.

Up the road we had a neighbor who was a black-smith. Sometimes he used to come down and watch us sweat. He never did sweat, but he'd watch us. In the winter time we'd have to knock holes in the ice to get water and wash off. We'd be cold.

He'd say, "Boy, how can you do that?"

Never did have our own neighbors sweat with us like that. When I was in grade school, some of the students who went to school with me would come by and watch us. After I got a little older some of my schoolmates— the ones on the basketball team—would come out and sweat.

Lot of times I used to sweat alone. I never had any father or grandfather there. My stepdad stayed for just a while. After my mother and him separated, he left. The man of the house builds the sweat house. After I got older, well, then I built the sweat house. Gathering all these teachings is like gathering rocks and different things. It's something that I grew up with.

Another way to sweat is called the mud bath. It's got to do with preparation, too. The ones I remember are preparing yourself to become a man, preparing yourself to take on responsibilities, becoming head of the household, and preparing yourself for marriage. It was done in about the same manner as the sweat house only it was out in the open. I guess it's kind of like a hot spring. You heat rocks to heat the water. When the water in the mud gets hot, sit in there and sweat. Mother Earth is the healer—Mother Earth and the water. Then you get out of there and you go in the cold water, just like you do at the sweat house. You sit out and rest a while and then go back in. This was done early in the morning. I did it with my stepfather. We were getting ready to go hunting. With a clean body the animals won't detect you by your smell. You can sneak right up on them. There were powers that you received from this way of preparation.

Sweating on Sunday, that was a no-no. Other reservations, other tribes, may do it, but it wasn't our way of life. A lot of times we'd sweat in the middle of the week. When I'd come home from school, somebody would be at the sweat house. I'd see the smoke and run and take my lunch pail to the house. Then I'd go to the sweat house. It was the place to go. I always felt good going there, because sometimes some of the old guys would happen to come by. They'd be passing by or come and live with us for awhile. They'd be preparing the sweat house and I wanted to be with them, see the old guys, and fix the sweat house.

A lot of men come there to sweat. I remember watching a man and his brother. One of them was married to my aunt. Both men had long hair, long braids. They were going on a hunting trip. They come and stayed with us. It must have been a week. They sweat everyday. I seen that myself.

The first day they come in to sweat both of them took

their rifles inside. It was because their rifles were given to them as keepsakes. They wouldn't say much. They just took the rifles in there and sweat with them. We'd go out of the sweat house and they'd take their guns out. They wouldn't just leave them laying in there. They'd take them out, set them up alongside of them while they went out to the creek and washed off. Then they'd sit outside there and talk by the creek until they went back inside. Each time they came out they'd bring their guns out. When they went back in, they'd take them in again. They did this all through that day of sweating.

They'd talk about hunting stories, hunting experiences they had, and how important it is to get game for the elder people. You go out and shoot a deer or elk and bring it home. The ladies are so happy to have this animal that they prayed for. Then they pray and thank the Creator for this.

When these two men got through sweating for the day, they'd take their rifles and clean them right there on the spot. They'd dry them up and really take good care of their guns—make sure they wouldn't get all rusted. Then they'd go on back to our house. The next day they didn't bring their guns.

They sweat like that for seven days. Of course, we didn't sweat on Sunday. Sunday was a day set aside for the Creator. You sing songs and give thanks to the Creator. The other days are The Old Man's days. You can clean yourself and prepare yourself for a certain journey just like these men were doing.

On the seventh day of their sweat, they took their guns back in. Each one of them had their rifle with him. On the first and last day, they talked about hunting, but all the other times they'd talk about different things.

Then they went hunting. I don't remember if they got anything or not.

You ask The Old Man to give you good eyesight, good vision, ask to keep healthy. Good, strong health so you don't get sick out there. This is talking to The Old Man, not talking to the Creator. You don't really ask, you say, "The Old Man is helping us . . . ."

Nowadays they call each one of these things a ceremony. I don't think this was. It was just part of life at the sweat house. So many things now are called ceremonies, but that wasn't the way I seen it. This is the way I feel about it yet.

One of the hunters was married and his wife passed away one winter. She was my aunt. They tried to get her to the hospital, but on the way she died. That following spring, he come and stayed with us. He come to clean himself. He talked about how he was starting to learn things. Once in a while he'd mention where he and his wife had been. He'd start remembering and talk to me about it. They had camped up in the mountains.

One day we got done sweating and he said, "We're gonna take a ride today."

We went way up above Grangeville. He said, "Three years ago we was here. We picked huckleberries."

We drove some more, took a side road, and stopped. We looked around and saw some old coffee cans they'd thrown away. He remembered a memory that was buried.

While he was sweating, he remembered a lot of things like that. His mind was getting cleared. He was what we call "letting go," letting his wife go. Sometimes we forget to do this. We forget and try to hang on to a loved one like you hang on to somebody if they wanted to leave the house. You grab them and pull them back. This is the illustration: Your mind won't let them go. You hang on and dwell on them like they were still there.

He came and cleared himself with sweats and then he left. He was a nice guy. I enjoyed having him around because he was talkative, but I never heard him speak of spirituality in the sweat house. Even the ones that were Christians that come there to sweat never sang their church hymns in the sweat house. They didn't offer the Lord's Prayer or anything like that. It's a different part of our way of life. That's the way I believe and that's the way I tell my children. It's important not to say anything against the other tribes. Each tribe has their own different ways. This is just the Nez Perce way.

Another time a man came up to our house to sweat. Why they used to come to ours — I guess it was a special place. Him and his wife had separated and he was feeling bad. His heart was broken. I seen him sitting out there getting ready to sweat. All of a sudden he started crying. That was something to me. It made me feel bad to see this.

He'd sweat just about every day. We had plenty of wood there and it was no problem. The first day I watched him get in the sweat house, he wouldn't say a lot of things in there.

The Old Man would help him. The last day he was free from all this. He felt different. He looked different. He didn't sit out there and cry. He was a happy person. The Old Man helped him feel good. Same way at the house. He'd laugh at the table. Before, he used to sit there and be quiet — not say much of anything. The last day there was a difference. He'd changed. It was just like a release. He stayed there about three weeks or so. That's another way The Old Man helps. I could see that myself.

I used to sweat a lot with my uncles down there at Culdesac. We had a sweat house along a nice creek there. It was part of Lapwai Creek. We used to have to cross a railroad track and a highway to go to the creek and the sweat house. Guys used to come and sweat before they'd go play baseball. Athletes, before a game, would sweat. Also, two guys and my uncle liked to play stick game. They'd prepare for their stick game by going to the sweat house. They'd sweat so many days and then maybe go to Nespelem or Pendleton.

They didn't bring anything in the sweat house that I can remember, but they'd talk and tell stick game stories and experiences. It was just like telling The Old Man all these things. I never heard them sing stick game songs in there. This is how it was in the old way.

I remember hearing them tell stories about one old man. He was a stick game player. He'd go play and take his horse and saddle with him. He'd be gone several days. Sometimes he'd come back with two or three horses or even a wagon full of stuff. When he got back, he'd go through this preparation of sweat again and maybe the next time he came back he'd be walking. He'd lose everything. But that's the way it was. He just happened to hit a bad streak. They didn't blame The Old Man for it.

These guys that told these stories would talk about whatever they were preparing for. They'd tell these kinds of stories in the sweat house. They'd tell each other about some of the winnings or the times they lost. Seems like they'd remember more things in there. Probably it was giving them more effect on their game. My uncles lived more of the Indian way of life than my grandmother. She was a Christian. Still, these men would come and stay with us.

It was an honor to sweat with the old men. They'd treat you so gentle. Most of the time they never gave you a lecture—not like "get on your case." The older gentlemen—the older, gentle people—knew you were young. They wouldn't try to abuse you by making it too hot in there. They'd ask you, "Is that too much?" I remember these things. I can practically name every one of them that was good that way.

This man who was crippled came to sweat. His legs probably had rheumatism or arthritis.

He told me, "Put on this pair of gloves and go make me some nettles."

He'd wrap about an inch and a half of nettles in a bundle. He'd bundle it up, wrap it, and tie it. While he was inside the sweat house I could hear him switching himself on the knees with that bundle of nettles.

I thought, "Boy, I bet that could hurt."

You know how it is when you touch a nettle—it burns. That was one of the things that was probably passed on to him by a medicine man or somebody. When he came out, he sat right there by the rocks. We'd sit around and talk, like a social gathering. When he'd go back in, he'd get that bunch of nettles and put it by him. When it started getting hot in there, he'd switch himself. You could hear it slapping. It would hurt. He'd do that two or three times. The last time he'd come out, he'd take that bundle of nettles and place it in the fire. He done this everyday. I'd make him a little bundle everyday, the same way everyday.

On the last day or so that we sweat, I could see him start to walk a little bit better. His knees loosened up. I'd see him packing his cane. He always took it with him. The last time he was walking pretty nice. When he was ready to leave, it seemed like happiness was in his heart. The Old Man had helped him.

When I got older—maybe about seven or eight years old, nine—I was sweating with this old man that was a warrior. He fought in the Nez Perce War, the 1877 War. He's the one that told me a lot of stories about my great-grandfather. They were very good friends. That's where I learned that my great-grandfather was a warrior and he fought. He told me stories about how brave my great-grandfather was, how good a shot he was, and all these things.

On the other side of Ferdinand, Mother's uncle had a place out there. She liked to go over there. This old man, Arthur, who fought in the War of 1877, lived with them. He had an Indian name, but I can't quite remember it now. They had a sweat house. I was about seven or eight years old when we'd go over and sweat with him. This old man never did speak, read, or write English, and he was already blind. I imagine he was in his eighties. He couldn't see, but he still wore these little wire-rimmed glasses. They were thick and rounded. He still wore them. Force of habit, I guess. I think he had become a Christian, because he had a haircut. His hair was short and white. He was the one who told me stories about my great-grandfather and the things he had done. He was a warrior. They had fought together.

He told me stories about my great-grandfather's bravery and power with horses. He would take an unbroken horse and lead it with his horse to a special place. Several days later, he'd come back riding the horse. He could also walk a circle around horses and they never crossed his path. They'd stay there all night just like they were in a corral. He was strong that way. He also told me how much of a sharpshooter he was and how my great-grandpa was a warrior with powers, too. I liked to help him. I'd grab his hand and lead him around.

He told me about being in the dark. He told me, "We're here in the dark in the sweat house. The Old Man makes it dark to give us more strength, more help. We come into the dark. Can't see anything so we have to close our eyes, because the sweat will run in our eyes and burn.

"We gotta close our eyes. That way we can concentrate more. Everything we talk about in here—the stories that we tell, the words that come out of our mouths—we're doing this with our eyes closed. Now when you go outside and you talk about something with your eyes closed, you can talk stronger."

Now this is something that I've learned from him. If you want to remember something, close your eyes. It can help you remember. You're sitting there with your eyes closed and it's helping you—all this time it's helping you.

This old man was strong.

He said, "Me, I'm in this dark all the time. I can't see anymore. I'm living in this dark world. That's why I can remember a lot of things. I don't get disrupted by live things running around, moving around. The only thing I see is what I remember."

This is true. If I want to remember something, I catch myself closing my eyes. I see a lot of people do that. Same way with sick people.

He told me, "Go visit somebody who's sick. You think they're asleep, but they've got their eyes closed and they're thinking about that pain. It doesn't seem like it hurts as much when you have your eyes closed."

I feel this is true, too. Strengthen your mind against pain. Close your eyes and just lay there. He had such a beautiful way of expressing things.

This old man, when he'd get you into the sweat house, would sweat really hot. He was a warrior and a strong, powerful man. He had a beautiful body. I admired it. He was lean, no fat or anything. Perfect, you know? He was old, but he had all these muscles. He'd sweat really hot. Leander and I would squirm around and get over by the door. We'd make little air holes where we could breathe. We'd stay in there as long as he did.

He would say, "Let's go out." Then he'd sprinkle water on the rocks.

"One for you, one for you, and one for The Old Man."

Each time he'd pour water on the hot rocks, we'd sit there until all that hot air settled down. It got nice and hot in there.

He'd say, "Okay, holler." Each time we come out we'd holler.

At night at the supper table we'd be sitting there eating and he'd always compliment us in front of all the people.

"This boy is tough. That sweat—pretty hot in there. He'd stay right there."

He didn't know we were cheating on him. He couldn't see. I guess us little boys had some old Indian tricks, too. He always made everybody believe how tough we were. Then we would look at each other like saying, "I guess we are tough."

One time we was sweating there and the rocks started steaming and boiling. It started getting real hot in there. Finally he told us in Indian, Let's get out! Let's get out! *hamtic'*. Hurry!"

We come out and there was a flash flood. We were in the middle of it. We waded out and were stuck there, because we didn't have any clothes. They got washed away. Finally somebody got concerned and came to see how we were. Here we were, sitting down there with no clothes. Downstream there was a fence we used to go across and that's where most of our clothes got hung up. They found his pants and he still had his money and his gold watch in his vest pocket. This old man, he was rich. He had lots of money. He had a money bag with a little snap on the top. It used to be full of silver dollars. It got to be a funny story after it was all over, but at the time it wasn't so funny.

One story I remember him telling us was about when he and the people were way up in the mountains on a huckleberry journey. Three, four, maybe five families met and set up a big camp. They went huckleberry picking where the ladies knew where to go, and the men went fishing from there. He was telling us this story inside the sweat house. One time they had a sweat house and it was a ways from camp. They had to walk down the trail. Down this trail was a nice creek and they built a sweat house. It was an old custom that the men sweat first and then when they'd come out the women would go in a little later in the evening. Most of the time it was dark by the time the women would come back to camp. They didn't have any lights or anything. Lights like flashlights were hard to come by in the old days, unless you had an old kerosene lantern.

On the way back from the sweat house, these women would experience something chasing them. It scared them. I guess this happened two or three times. They were talking about it and this man heard them. He was sitting by the fire and he listened to them talk. He was a lot younger then and he had good eyes.

He said, "You ladies sweat and then I'll go down there

and sweat by myself. Then I'll come back by myself in the dark."

He did that. When he got through sweating, he felt around and put his clothes on. He got up the trail a little ways and he heard something. It got closer and started to walk behind him. It was coming closer. When he was really close he turned and hollered at it, "Go away!"

He turned around and saw this little old owl fly up.

He laughed and said, "Oh, it was just an owl."

It kept following everybody that would come out of there. It was a little owl and he hopped along behind everybody. It sounded like footsteps. They all laughed and they weren't scared anymore. That's what his illustration was about, to not get scared.

What it means to take care of The Old Man: Make sure sacks and things are cleaned. Wash them out and hang them up. Take your rocks and set them outside by the door so the sun will hit them. It gets damp inside. Make your own wood. Just take care of him and he will take care of you.

Maybe you find an old chair or something. You take it and give it to The Old Man—that's part of his property. Tools, pitchfork, all kinds of things. You say, "I'm going to take this to The Old Man, to the sweat house, so he has all these possessions. Some of these things could be old blankets or old quilts. It feels like part of your family. That's the way I still feel about it.

My wife, Andrea, tells me, "Why do you get this and why do you get that?"

I say, "Well, someday that's for the sweat house."

Things that happened in the sweat house are all good memories, because I learned so much about the Indian way of life and what it means.

Just before the War of 1877, the Nez Perces already had big herds of horses. They already had a lot of cattle. They already knew how to do these things. I don't know why the government was trying to make our people change. They were trying to make them different. Eventually we Nez Perce lost all this. They took away all our horses and cattle. Our ancestors spent a lot of their lives raising these horses and cattle. They had them when they were made to leave their beautiful homeland in the Wallowas.

They also lost a lot along the way because of the rivers they had to cross and the mountains they had to go over. It was difficult. My grandmother remembers hanging on to her mother riding in the saddle. She was six years old at the time. She was hanging on to her mother from behind, traveling at night. They hardly ever traveled at night. She also remembers hearing gun-

To Kill Us

shots. She remembers hearing people cry, seeing people laying on the ground, and fire and smoke.

They were all full-blooded Nez Perces and they all believed in the spirituality. They had their powers that they used and all the other categories that we have—the sweat house, The Old Man, the animals that give power through the *weyekin*. They had medicine men and medicine women there. They had everything right there. I know that Chief White Bird was a medicine man. They had it all together and that's why they were so strong and went so far. They had put all these things together by understanding one another—what one could do to help the others. They relied on one another. They come to a certain problem or a certain thing and they knew who to go to for the right direction.

I have it in my mind to see all the places our people went through in 1877. I had the opportunity to do the opening prayer for a dedication in the little town of Winifred, Montana. It gave me a chance to speak about the Nez Perce people. The Nez Perces went through there in 1877. They went through there on their way from the Yellowstone area. Then they crossed the Missouri River down there at Cow Island. I've heard stories about this place.

I said, "We didn't go through there to settle in that area. We were going through there to save our traditions, our culture, our language, our religion. We wanted to take it someplace where we could use it like we always did with peace and harmony to Mother Earth."

There must have been sixty people there for the dedication. And they understood. With my own eyes I got to see Cow Island. This man, Tom, took my wife, my granddaughter, and me out there. The tour was called off that day because it rained. This place, when it gets a little muddy, becomes very slick. The mud becomes gumbo. So they called the trip off that day. Tom said, "I have a four-wheel drive rig and you've come a long ways." I couldn't refuse his offer. He could probably see I was disappointed we weren't going to get to go out there. We talked a lot about my people. He and his wife were nice and very understanding.

I had it pictured in my mind as a rocky, bluff area like the Snake River and Salmon River areas, but it was different. There's a lot of hills and a lot of deep valleys in there. Somehow the people made their way down through there and got to the bottom of the Missouri River and went across. Of course, there are some war stories that are interpreted by people in a lot of different ways: some for the people of the Nez Perce and some for the people of the United States Army and for the fur traders that were already settling there. It will always be that way.

First, the Nez Perce people wanted to get food. I don't know, they had some misunderstanding with the townspeople and there was a skirmish. All they wanted was food. After being chased and fought with, they probably took food and supplies. They wanted to kill us. We don't respect one another too highly when we're in a war. In any war there's always women, children, and everything, being destroyed. Destruction runs high. I've seen all this destruction with my own eyes. Why do we have to destroy one another? It's really hard to speak about the wars because we all know what it does. We all know how badly we treat one another.

We weren't looking for war. They call it the War of 1877. I have my own thoughts about that. I don't see how they could call it a war when we weren't the ones at war. We were trying to get away. We were trying to protect ourselves. When you're being chased like that you run for your life. And this is what we were doing. The way I understand it is the government wanted to take our land, no matter what tribe, and put us together in one place where they could control everything. They would take over the land, develop it, and use it the way they wished. And a lot of this happened. Our non-treaty Indians really wanted to save the language because the government was trying to take it away. That's in the history books. They wanted to take away our religion. That's also in the books. And they wanted to take a lot of other things away, especially our freedom. And that's also in the books.

So this is what the people were trying to do: save all

this and take it somewhere where they could do these things without being told how to do it. But they put us all together on a reservation and denied us the right to speak our language and to use our religion.

A lot of the veterans were allowed to come back to their homeland if they agreed to become Christians. I guess that was the purpose, to stamp out the Indian religion. You could see that. Other chiefs and bands were made to sing and worship out of books. They listened to one man do all the talking and they didn't want to do it that way. I think that's one of the reasons for the War of 1877. You can look at it from either side. I can, because I grew up Presbyterian. I watched and practiced it.

Now I have my own thoughts about freedom of religion. A lot of times I sit here and think about the war. How different it was. When you get shot at, get abused, see your relations and your children get killed, then that starts stirring up a lot of strong negative feelings toward your enemies. Then you become enemies. That's why I have this negative thought about it being called the War of 1877, because we weren't trying to make war.

That's another thing that doesn't happen now. A lot of us know one another and the feelings aren't that way. Again, modern times has changed the attitudes of the Nez Perces. We are being split every day by new things coming into the world. If we had to live again like our old people did, I don't know how many of us could make it. It would be pretty hard.

I've been to Oklahoma where the people were sent after they surrendered. I met a man named Felix at the Tonkawa Reservation. He was an elder. My wife, my grandson, and I just happened to meet him there. We took this journey because my grandson was going to a workshop at Oklahoma University. Also, there was a powwow at the same time in Oklahoma City. It was called the Red Earth Powwow.

So when I found out we were going, I got prepared. I told my wife what my plan was. Seems like I always come up with a plan of some kind. I asked her how much dried traditional food she had in our house that we could take along. She looked around and come up with dried elk and deer meat, dried salmon, *qaws*, *qemes*, dried huckleberries, chokecherries, and some mountain tea. I told her to put each one in a different bundle.

On our way we went to White Bird, Idaho. When we got to White Bird, I asked her to stop. I had a gallon coffee can. We stopped where we could see down into the battleground and I got a bucket of dirt from Mother Earth. I put it in the van and then we went on. We got down to Rapid River, Idaho, our ancient fishing grounds, and I went to the creek and got a jar full of water. I wanted to do this sacred thing for the people that had been exiled in Oklahoma. The preparations that I made were, to me, like what we do for the Root Feast every year. And these people were people of my tribe, the Nez Perce. They believed in and survived by all the sacred elements I gathered—and the way they used the foods, most of them being dried.

When we got to Ponca City, Oklahoma, near the Tonkawa Tribe, Felix told me the history of what happened there after the Nez Perce people had been sent back—most of them not to where they wanted to go. Some went to the reservation. Some went up to Colville, Washington.

There was a burial place where many of our people were buried. In later years, a farmer purchased that piece of ground where the burial places were and he pushed all the stone markers into the creek and covered them up. Then he plowed over the gravesite and used it for farming. All three of us shed tears.

If I went and bought a piece of land from, say, a non-Indian, or a white man, and there was a grave on it, I know I wouldn't do these things. The soul and the body of a person has high priority. His resting place is like a landmark. And I'm very positive that I wouldn't treat it the way some of my ancestors have been treated. But I guess respect is much stronger and more spiritually minded in the Indian people, because of the way our people have respect for Mother Earth. This again is something that was put into my heart when I was a little boy. It still remains that I give concern to the people that have already gone. I will do my best to make my younger people understand these things.

Finally, I guess, the government decided to fence off a little square about the size of my yard—50' x 100' or something like that—and build a nice-looking fence around it. In the middle there was a monument with words about what this particular monument was about. But Felix said, "Don't believe what you read there, because that isn't the way it was."

I can't remember the exact words that were written on there because it didn't mean that much to me. A burial ground had been destroyed. I didn't know it was like that. I thought I would take my things there and put them close to the cemetery where the people were. I was going to have a little ceremony there myself—a blessing or whatever you want to call it. Maybe, in some way, wherever these people were buried, the ground they were buried in would be sacred. I felt the connection with the food and the elements—the water—would somehow be felt by the spirits, that they would remember the things done in the past to strengthen our souls, our minds, and our bodies each year. Maybe some of these children never got to taste the sacred foods of our homeland. The elders were probably heartbroken because they didn't have these foods. This is the reason I did this: Because I'm connected to the old ways with the religion. I strongly feel the need for these things to happen this way.

So I did this: I paced off seven steps. I faced the east and dug this trench. I laid down some of my dirt that I brought from White Bird Battleground. Then I took some of the water from Rapid River and sprinkled it over the dirt and I placed all these traditional foods in order—the same order that we use in the Root Feast. And after I had placed them like that, I sang my song. Then I covered them up with my dirt and I blessed them with water again. My grandson, my wife, and I sang another song. I spoke my language to the Creator to give forgiveness. I didn't even know who did this. But I asked for forgiveness for him—for whoever.

Things like this should be done because the people were being chased from their homeland. We have already done this at the Big Hole battle site. Maybe, in some way, the spirits will make it more comfortable where the people are. I hope that this doesn't cause any hard feelings with anybody. It does make a stronger feeling for me, especially as a leader in the Long House. I hope to someday do this at the Bear Paw site. Someday I want to make a special trip with my Long House people over there and do this. To do this I will feel complete.

Mother Earth is taking care of the people now. They live by the spirits. The food was important to their lives. They survived by these foods and the water and the songs. I know a lot of them didn't have a burial the way we bury our dead. They never had the chance. So this is my own way of connecting them with the past. Most of these things that I do always come from the thoughts of how I would honor the dead, how I would honor the people. How you honor Mother Earth and how you ask the Creator—maybe, in some way, the forgiveness is stronger. Maybe the hurt will not hurt as much. Maybe love and freedom will spread to the future and make room for better things. That's the reason I do these things.

In 1977, we were invited to go to the celebration at Fort Belknap, Montana. The Gros Ventre and Assiniboin tribes of Fort Belknap invited us to come over there because each year they had a Chief Joseph Memorial Powwow. The Bear Paw battlefield is close to their reservation. That was the year it was the 100th anniversary of the 1877 War, so they had a special pow-wow for that. My father was getting very blind and very sick. I told him where we were going and that his grandfather, my great-grandfather was buried there. I asked him if he wanted to go along.

He said, "I would. Even though I can't see good I still want to feel that I'm close to the land where my grandfather's buried."

He told me all these things in the Nez Perce language. So we went. My children danced and he stayed at the motel. Then on Sunday, they had the special ceremonies out at the battlefield. I took him out there for the pipe ceremony and drumming and singing, but he stood to the side. Afterwards I showed him where the surrender site was. We didn't want to walk him over there, but I pointed to the direction. I explained the way the hills were and how the trails were. I explained all this in my language to him. Then I explained about how big the area was and described just about how it looked so he could envision it in his mind. And then it made him feel sad.

He said, "I've always wanted to come here and I never have. I feel good that I'm here. I feel good that I feel close to where his body is. My grandpa is here somewhere. I've heard a lot of stories about my grandfather. He must have been a very strong man."

I don't know how old my great-grandfather was when he got killed, but my father remembered the stories he was told about his grandfather. He told me some of them things right there on that spot. When you feel the strength of another person, some of these stories and things are revealed without any hesitation because they want to talk about it. This is what he did right there when he was standing by our car. Everybody else was mingling around doing other things, but he stood there with me and told me these things. Some of the things he would hesitate about. I knew it was hurting him to speak like that. He told me a lot of things right there.

We come on home after that observance was over, because I had to work. My father became sicker and sicker. We took him to the hospital and the doctor put him right in. I was working nightshift at the sawmill and I went to see him one afternoon. He used to do so many things to help me with my job. He'd always worry about my pickup. In the fall time he'd always say, "Well son, better go down and buy some studded tires. Better get the antifreeze." He'd always remind me. I knew what to do, because he was always telling me.

We sat there and talked a lot about these things in the hospital. Just him and me. We always talked in our language.

He said, "What time is it?"

I told him it was getting close to three, about a quarter to three.

"Well, you better get home and lay down."

I used to do that all the time when I was working nightshift. About three o'clock, if I was doing something outside, I'd come in and just lay down. Sometimes I'd sleep. Sometimes I wouldn't. I always had that hour of relaxation before Andrea had my supper ready at 4:00 every day.

I said, "I guess I will. I'll come back down tomorrow."

"Okay, okay."

I started for the door and he called me back.

"Oh, just a minute," he said. So I came back. There was something in his room he wanted me to bring down to him.

I said, "Okay."

I was getting ready to go, then he stuck his hand out. He wanted to shake hands. He never did that before. We shook hands and we laughed. And I left.

I went home and laid down. Went on to work that night and during noon hour, when I was in the cafeteria, I got this call from my boss who was up in the sawmill. He told me I better go ahead and go home because my father just died. I think that was on the 19th of October.

Things run through your mind about last words or last conversations. In that month of October he told me so many things. I think he knew what he was doing. He told me strong words about Indian people, the old instructions the old people had, and the old ways of discipline. I never recorded any of it. Maybe I should have, but it's all in my mind and in my heart. I know what he meant. Some of the things that he told me were like a little puzzle, but now I'm solving them.

He was a veteran, a warrior. He spent thirty-two months overseas during WWII. He was a leader, an elder. In my way of life now, I have to let him go. Let him rest.

Warriors
and War

World War II took a lot of young people. Young men, mostly. In 1943, everybody that was my age thought about wanting to go. I couldn't get in, so I raised my age one year. I told my mother I wanted to go.

She said, "Well, you better finish school."

But you know how it is when you have something on your mind. I finished the eleventh grade, signed up for the draft, and got my papers. Before I went into the service, I went to this rock that was on the hillside near our home. It was my favorite place and has a lot of meaning to me. I would go to this place to get myself together, meditate, or communicate with my Creator. I've done this a lot while I was growing up. The rock is on the hillside, a little bit above the trees—not too far from where our sweat house used to be. The fence line is right next to it. There are several big, white rocks, but what makes this one stand out is it's the biggest rock. It sits on top of all the other sand rocks. It's a good feeling there. The wind blows through the trees and makes a nice sound, like a song. Up on the prairie you get a lot of wind.

I must've spent two hours up there by myself. I guess I was saying, "I want to come back again." I knew I was going to go away and it was really my first time away from home, this land where I spent all my life. That's why I went up there. I thought a lot about what would happen if I didn't come back. My eyes would not see this place. It was sad to feel this. I was not making any predictions about my life. I felt prepared. Right, or good, or bad—whatever. I tried to find direction up there. Asking direction about the way to go on with my life.

Along with that, my grandaunt, *Tuklaʃanmy*, was already ailing. She had breast cancer. I visited with her before I went to the rock. She told me I would be back. She said, "You have strong blood."

She also told me, "Your great-grandfather was a warrior. He died during battle. He died with bravery. You'll probably have a lot of things happen to you. Things happen. Don't get discouraged. For one thing you're going to get very homesick This is your first time leaving home."

She warned me about that.

"But when you have a home like you have, the way you grew up, think about them different places, your favorite places. The rock is especially your own place."

The home place—homestead, I guess you call it. The trails I used to follow and the places I used to play all had strong meaning to me.

Then she said, "You think about all this when you're lonely or homesick. You'll make it all right."

I could tell she knew a lot about the land. My grandaunt had a strong background, strong spiritual feelings because she was a medicine woman. A lot of the Indian people had their own special places. A lot of them still do. Some of the people go to the known places where Indians used to get their powers, what they call *weyekin*.

She said, "I watched you. I watched you grow up. I watched you do a lot of things. You'll be back. I want you to know that I will always remember you every day in my way. I'm getting pretty weak now. But I always think of you—all of you, every day—even though I have to go away from this land when my time comes."

She gave me all these good instructions about bravery because of my elders, because of what they had to do to protect this sacred land—this land we loved. She told me to go and remember all these little places. So that's why I went to the rock after visiting with her.

The time was getting close and I didn't know I was going to leave until the day before I left. I went to

Grangeville to meet with all the other inductees to go to Spokane for a physical. All of us gathered around the bus parked right in the middle of the street in Grangeville. They had a big band playing. People were sad. A lot of lives were being lost during the war. That's where I always think about bravery. In the beginning, it was my mother. Even though I was the only child she ever had, she was strong. She was always smiling, and with her eyes, showing she loved me.

In Spokane, an officer swore us into the army. We had seven days to go back home and take care of business. My mother took me around to different places to tell my relatives I was going away. I went to see my aunt in Kamiah. I told her I was going to leave the following Monday or Tuesday.

She said, "I'm going outside now. I want to see you out there pretty soon."

I talked to other people and then I went outside. She was standing outside the gate by the car. She motioned me to come over. I went over and she told me a lot of things. It all boiled down to my great-grandfather, about how he was strong in his ways. Courageous. A well-behaved person, strong in his religion—the old religion. That's why he was in the war. He was remembered as a person that had a lot to do with horses. She also told me that there were a lot of our people, even in the old times, that were afraid.

She said, "I don't want you to be like that. Lot of them even went as far as to turn against their own people by helping out the United States Army. I don't want you to do that. I want you to be like your great-grandpa. I want you to be brave."

She told me about some of our own people "Our men were supposed to be brave, but they all weren't brave."

I guess there were some that put on buckskin dresses in the nighttime and rode away, making others believe they were women leaving. They were afraid to go fight in the war.

"I don't want you to be like that. Follow in the footsteps of your old warriors and be proud." She held out her hand to shake my hand.

She said, "It may be hard going away now."

I felt something in my hand and I put it in my pocket. In our Nez Perce language we don't have a word for good-bye. Later, I felt in my pockets and I said, "I got some money here."

I looked and it was two fifty-dollar bills. That wasn't the first time she done that.

I visited different places and strong people — and it all goes with you. You don't just leave it all behind, it all goes wherever you go. I left the house that morning and I went to Grangeville. Grandmother and Mother were the only ones at the house.

My grandmother instructed me, "Always eat a good breakfast. You may not get a chance to eat for the rest of the day."

I had my big breakfast. I was told by the recruiters not to bring a bunch of things. Everything was going to be furnished. "Take just what you have on." That's the way I went.

I said to Grandma and Mother, "*Waaqo kusa*. I'm going to leave."

They both sat there and told me to take care of myself. Grandmother smiled at me and so did Mother. They didn't want to make me feel bad, I guess. They knew how important it was for me to go. I told them to leave my dogs in the house. They were both sleeping by the woodstove.

"Don't let them out. I'll catch the bus and I'll be gone."

Later my mother told me she let the dogs out and they run all over. They were gone for a while and then came back, ran upstairs to see if I was up there, and ran back down. They scratched on the door to go out and she let them out again. She heard they went into town to look for me. Soon as the dogs got back, they ran upstairs to see if I was up there. They gave up for a while, then for several days they'd run upstairs early in the morning to see if I was there.

I stayed the night in Grangeville and about seven the next morning I caught the bus. We had to come clear back through my hometown, Ferdinand, on our way to Lewiston. When we got to the post office, where the bus used to stop, I looked out the window and there were all my classmates waving at me. The basketball coach was there, too. They were right there giving me encouragement. It was nice to see that.

There was another bus behind us taking in the local passengers. My mother got on there. She wanted to come into Lewiston where I was going to leave from. The bus terminal was at the old Raymond Hotel. That afternoon, they loaded us up into three big Greyhound buses. Mom never let me see her cry.

"After I get my basic training, I'll be back to see you and Grandma."

A lot of the other ladies were crying. They had sons there. I got on the bus and waved. I felt good and strong inside. I met a couple of Coeur d'Alene Indian boys who were going. They became real good friends of mine.

We went across the Clarkston Bridge and I said, "Well, I guess we're on our way."

When we got outside of Clarkston, Washington, it got real quiet. Before that, people had been talking. All of a sudden it got quiet. It was the first time, for a lot of us, to leave home. I'd been away to Seattle and Portland, but this was a little bit different. Going away and not knowing where you were going or when you were coming back—if you were coming back. It was a sad ride from Lewiston, Idaho, to Pendleton, Oregon.

In Pendleton, we had our first encounter with the men with the stripes—the sergeants and all that. They ordered us around and we learned how to take orders. They told us where to line up and what to do. They gave us some of them commands that I became familiar with later in army life. At the time I didn't know what they were talking about. I don't think any of us did.

The train came and we listened for our names to be called. We answered and then got on the train. They assigned us a place to sit. We ate and then we spent our first night away from home in a Pullman car. All night long you could heard the clickety-clack of the train. We'd come through some town and you could hear the railroad crossing bell ringing, "Bing, bing, bing." We went by and didn't know where we were at. You try to sleep and it's hard.

They woke us all up in the morning and fed us. We sat there the rest of the day, just riding. It was a quiet ride. Oh, a few people came by and talked to me, but I didn't know anybody really close. I had to get acquainted, but I've always had a knack for that. Ever since I was a little fella. So one of the first things I did was make friends, because I knew we shouldn't make enemies amongst ourselves when we were going to go to war together.

We come through Pocatello, Idaho, and some other

places. We asked each other "Where did you go to school?" and what sports we played. We was all about the same age. Some of us even played ball against each other. We didn't talk too much about home. That was a sore spot in everybody's mind. So we asked, "I wonder where we're going?" or "What kind of outfit are we going to be in?" Anything. We really didn't know.

Finally, we found out we were going to Fort Douglas, Utah. It was an induction center. We were on the train all night and all day. We pulled up at the railroad station and they unloaded us into an army truck. They piled us in there and closed the back canvas door. We couldn't see out. They drove us away. About half an hour later we pulled up and stopped at the main gate. The MP gave us the high sign and we were in Fort Douglas, Utah.

Seems like every time we turned around they were calling roll call. We went into the barracks and saw the army bunks and army blankets. Everything was the same. We had to get acquainted with the whole setup. I didn't have any experience with this—not even the Boy Scouts. They didn't have anything like that at home. Some of the other Indian people were probably familiar with some of these military commands and things, because back in the old days the Indian schools had discipline like the army. They had to wear little uniforms. But I never had any of that experience at all. Everything was new to me.

That night they put us to bed and turned the lights off. It got real quiet. That's when I heard people sobbing and crying under the covers. It brought me back to all the words that were spoken to me before I left home.

"Be brave. Be strong."

They give me all these Indian words. "Don't get lonesome if you can help it." I remembered all these things and I could even picture the people's faces who were telling me these things that kept me brave. I don't know how many people slept that night, but I went to sleep.

I was pretty much used to getting up early, but it seems like we only slept about ten minutes and then they turned the lights on again: "Everybody rise and shine! Hit the deck!" or whatever. How were we going to shine? Some guys were still stretching around there.

They blew the whistle and said, "Everybody line up out there!"

We had to run down there. Some of them guys didn't even have their shoes on. That's when you start learning how. They wake you up and you start getting dressed right now, because your day has started.

We had to fall out on the street for roll call again. Even if they knew we were all there, they still got to have roll call—what they call, reveille. After we got finished with that, we had to come back and mop our floor. The place wasn't even dirty and we had to mop it anyway. That's just a routine. That's the way you start training. I started right there. We had time to go to the shower room and the wash room to clean up. They told us to do all this and get ready for "chow." It wasn't breakfast, dinner, or supper. It was always, "chow." I learned that word pretty easy. It wasn't homecooking. I realized that. You didn't have to eat this chow, but then you would have starved.

After we ate, we had to sit around and wait and wait until it was time for us to start processing. We had medical and dental examinations. We got some shots. The whole bit. It was fun, to start with. It was new. Next thing, they lined us up again and marched us down to the barber shop to get crew cuts.

I had made friends with some Indian boys from

Burns, Oregon. Two of them had braided hair like I got now. I tell you one thing, they looked different when they come out of that barbershop. I don't know what they done with the hair. If it would've been me, I would've had the braids sent home. I don't know what they done with theirs. One young man cried when he had his cut off. And I understand now why he cried. The only time we are allowed to cut our hair is when our wife or our mother dies. If you have long braids, that's when you cut your hair.

We got all done with our hair cuts and our shots and everything. Back to the mess hall for chow. We finished and sat around the barracks and waited for the whistle again. Finally, the whistle blew and down the stairs we went, just as fast as we could go. They only allowed us so many seconds to get down there. We found our spot and lined up.

They marched us over to the supply room and we got all our gear—our uniforms, shoes, socks, field jackets, and caps—just the basic things. They gave us a bag to put our own civilian clothes in and we dragged that along with all the others. When we come out of there we were dressed as soldiers. We all laughed at each other for the way we looked. It was funny. The jacket (they called it a blouse) had brass buttons all the way down—buttons all over. All of us looked different. We went on our way, ready to hit the road.

After we got our uniforms, they gave us a bunch of wrapping paper and told us to wrap all our things up and send them home—all our own clothes. That's what we did for the rest of the day. I had a real nice black leather jacket that I bought when I worked that one summer before I left. It was kind of a trend in them days to wear a black jacket, white corduroy pants, engineer boots, and a hat. It was like a hunting cap. I had a green one made out of that same material, except our high school colors were green and white. I sent all that to my friend, Jesse. We had the same birthday, but I'm two years older than him. I call him my little brother. Later, he went into the navy.

There we were, all uniformed and all our clothes sent away. They told us to sit around and wait until we got orders. Seemed like it was hours and hours and hours.

Then they told us, "Come and saddle up." That meant "get packed." We packed and carried our bags with our names and serial numbers on them. Mine was 3946249. We were there about five days. They had to clear us out because they was another bunch coming through. All our stuff was down on the street, beside us. Roll call again. We got on the truck, the flap was shut, and we went down to the train depot. Same thing all over again. We got on the troop train and sat there for what seemed like a couple hours before the train started moving.

We didn't know where we were going. We didn't know what direction we were going. Seems like we rode for two nights—it was a long time. We could see out, but none of us really knew where we were at, because we had never been away before. We tried to find out where we were going. Nobody would tell us.

All of a sudden somebody said, "We're in Texas." Wow, Texas.

We stopped and they told us to get off. We piled out. "Back out. Line up."

Soon as we were getting out, a fighter plane flew right over us. We didn't know what we were getting into. We thought it was the Air Force. I guess that was wishful thinking.

"Hey, we're going to get in the Air Force!"

"Oh, I don't think so."

"Where are we at?"

We didn't know. We finally found out we were at a place called Camp Swift, Texas. That was about fifty miles from Austin. It was a real small town called Bastrup, Texas. It was February and not really warm, yet. We got on a great, big, long bus and went to the base. That's where we met our captain. Our commanding officer welcomed us. They separated us.

"You go this way and you go that way."

He told us we were in the 529th Engineers, Light Pontoon Company, Floating Bridge Builders. The 529th guys lined up on one side and across the street was the 511th Light Equipment Company. Everything started coming into focus. I was learning how to march and drill. All the things that we were going to use, like, discipline, we were doing. We had to march, do close-order drill, take hikes, calisthenics—just about everything for thirteen weeks. Then, after thirteen weeks of basic training, we went into advanced training. I don't know why everything is thirteen. In advanced, we learned bridge building and things like demolition.

The first two weeks there, we were quarantined. We couldn't go out of our barracks area or the other part of the camp like the theaters or the PX. (That was the Post Exchange where you could buy pop, candy, beer, and things like that.) But we could send somebody—a representative from each barracks—to go to the store. Luckily, I had a few dollars with me since my aunt gave me some money. Right away there were poker games and crap games. I always wanted to play from the first day.

We had to learn the chain of command—our cadre—

the personnel that was going to be in charge of us. We had sergeants, a squad leader, a commanding officer, platoon officers, and platoon sergeants. I tried to learn all these things. The captain who was our commanding officer was a graduate of Louisiana State University. He must've been 6'3" or 6'4," built like a superman. He stood so straight and made us all feel good to be under his command. He was well-mannered, taught us good, and talked to each one of us like he'd known us for a long time.

If there was something he had to repeat he'd always say, "I told you once and I will tell you a*gain*." That was his word.

In the camp area, we'd march down the rows. Everybody was in step, marching along. Pretty soon he had us all singing.

He'd tell us to, "Sound off."

We started to get into the flow of it.

At the PX you could buy things so much cheaper. Candy was a nickel a bar. A bottle of beer was ten cents. If you wanted to get a little classier and drink eastern beer, well, it was fifteen cents a bottle. If you were in the service, you were eligible to drink alcohol. At home, Indians weren't allowed to buy or drink liquor. That was a federal law. When we got into the service it didn't matter. I felt a little backward at first when I started learning to drink beer.

I'd step up and say kinda hesitant, "I want a bottle of beer."

"What'd you say?"

Then louder, "I want a bottle of beer."

That privilege felt strange. I guess it was the uniform and being in the army. In Austin there were places where no questions were asked like "What nationality are you?" They served you.

We had to do things like go to the dentist. Instead of deadening your jaws they'd grab you by the back of the head and hold you to the chair. Then it was just drill away.

They didn't ask you, "Does that hurt?" Just go to work on you.

The first day I had to have one or two fillings. I was fortunate. Some of them had to go back three or four times. They told this one guy he had to go back to the dentist. The next day he wasn't in his bunk. He was gone. Took off.

We had to take eye checks. Everybody that needed glasses got glasses. They were pulling us all together. We needed good eyesight to qualify for riflemen or sharpshooters. Before we went out on the rifle range, we had to have all this training on how to hold the rifle to your cheek and how to squeeze the trigger. I knew all this already because my stepdad was a WWI veteran and he showed me a lot of these things. He used to tell me stories in the sweat house. He talked about close-order drill, marching, and things like that. So I had a good idea about what was happening.

About every day they had rifle inspection, and some of these guys wouldn't even be able to handle a rifle. They lined you up in ranks and the commander took the gun out of your hand. If it passed inspection he'd say, "Okay" and give it back. That was teaching us to keep our rifles clean at all times.

Some of these poor guys were not qualifying on the rifle range. They were the ones that were afraid of guns. They were having a hard time. We named this one guy

"Red Ryder." He was deathly afraid of guns. He used to come all to pieces when we had to be out on the firing line. They had to take him out on the firing range on Saturday or Sunday afternoon, instead of going to town, to try to get him to qualify.

This one time, an officer went out there to get him to qualify and he was getting pretty frustrated, like when you feel you're being forced to do something. Red Ryder got out there, got the gun all loaded, and somehow pulled the trigger and shot a hole in the jeep tire. He was nervous. This made the lieutenant pretty upset. He told him to change the tire. Red Ryder didn't mind that.

He said, "I can do that alright."

He changed the tire and this time he parked the jeep quite a ways away so he wouldn't hit the tire again. Luckily, it was the tire and not something else. They must've took him out there four weekends in a row and he finally qualified. This built up his confidence. He never did tell us why guns affected him like that.

All he'd say was, "I never been around guns that much."

You get over in a foreign country, in a war, and you don't want him getting all shook up and shoot you in the back accidentally. He might have to save your life someday. We learned everything about rifles, .30 caliber machine guns, demolition, land mines, hand grenades, dynamite, different kinds of poisonous gases, bazookas, and flame throwers. Still, at night, you could hear sobbing. Some of them just couldn't help it.

I remembered the words that were told to me, "Be brave. Be strong. Be careful."

The things people tell each other, going into something like that, are words spoken from the heart. About this time, I started corresponding with my father. He was in the service and already overseas. He was in the service for about a year before I went in. He wrote home to somebody for my address. I was surprised to get a letter from him. I always knew he was my father, but I never had that relationship with him. When the letter came I went to the barracks and sat on my bunk. He sent a picture of himself and at the top of the letter it said, "Dear Son." He never really called me that before. I wrote back to him and told him where I was.

The next time around he sent a letter about his training. He said, "Learn everything you can. What you're learning over there you'll use when you cross the ocean. Be serious about this training. It's very important. Some things might bore you, but don't turn your back on any of it."

We wrote back and forth and I began to develop a relationship with him. I got to learn a lot from him just corresponding with him. The picture he sent helped me in my army life. I'd look at the picture and say, "This is my dad." It would be a long time before we could really spend some time together.

When we weren't training and taking classes after classes, they had orientation for all of us. They told us what was going on in Europe. I liked that because I met people who worked in foreign lands. In the army there were people from all walks of life. We had one guy who was a college graduate. Later there were guys who couldn't read or write. The service was getting desperate for men. I got to be a Motor Pool Dispatcher and was responsible for taking care of a lot of equipment. It was fun. I became a corporal and got $66.00 a month.

Our outfit was getting all together and we started building bridges.

The little town of Bastrup, Texas, was a small community of Blacks, Hispanics, and Whites. Many of us came from the Northwest and we had a hard time adapting to the way of life they had down there. We weren't accustomed to the segregation they had back in that time. I mean, it was sad to see this. The black people (back then the term was "colored") had their own part of town. They always had their own side of the street to walk on. They had their own drinking fountains. You could see the sign at the drinking fountain "For Colored People Only." They had their own little places to hang out, like taverns. On the weekends we'd go on pass and it was especially crowded. It was hard to obey the segregation rules and this caused us to get in fights.

One time we were coming back from a pass. There were maybe twelve of us together and we got on the bus and sat down. One guy, a person from the South, got on. About halfway down the aisle, a black soldier was passed out across the seat. He must've had a little too much to drink. His head was sticking out over the seat into the aisle. The guy that got on the bus saw the soldier laying across there and he didn't like it.

"You belong in the rear," he hollered at him.

The soldier was passed out. The guy went and kicked him in the head. We were not used to seeing that. All hell broke loose. We had quite a battle there, but all the black people had to ride in the rear of the bus. It was something new for us to see—to treat another human being that way. We all got reprimanded. It was my first experience going in front of the captain and he was from the South.

He said, "Maybe some day something will be done

about it. I went to LSU and I learned a lot of things up north. I saw different things. I don't know why this has to keep going on and on this way."

They had us segregated. There were black companies there. A black battalion was clear across the street from us. We used to hear them. We liked to listen to them march. We'd even get out there and watch them whenever we had the chance. They looked like they were having a lot of fun. A lot of those soldiers were from the North, too, and they had a hard time adjusting to the ways of the southern people. The way the white people treated them didn't set right with me. I don't think it set right with all my comrades from my outfit. One of the fellow members of my outfit was hit by some guy from the 102nd Ozark Division. When he came to, he remembered seeing the Ozark Division patch of the guy that hit him. After that, every time he'd see an Ozark patch he started a fight.

In Louisiana, we built a few roads and repaired a few roads. When our maneuvers were pretty much winding down, our lieutenant—in appreciation for our somewhat good behavior—planned an event. He was a pretty nice guy. Everybody liked him because he was just like one of the boys. When we got into town he gave us instructions.

He said, "I want everybody here at midnight. We'll go back to camp."

Everybody went and done their thing, went to the movies. Of course, a lot of us went to the little taverns that they had around there. Some of us came back to the truck a little bit early. Everybody was having a good time and somebody pulled out a pair of dice and we started having a big dice game. Pretty soon the MPs come by. Our lieutenant was right in there with us—he was playing dice, too. We were going pretty good and the MPs come and told us that we weren't allowed to do that on the streets of Leesville, Louisiana. Our lieutenant pulled his rank on the MPs. They left. Pretty soon they came back with a lieutenant colonel and that's when things happened.

The lieutenant colonel ordered the MPs to search our truck and they found a lot of liquor bottles in there. They confiscated all of them. They made the lieutenant open each one and pour them down the drain. On the way back he said, "I've never been that sad in all my life to see all that liquor going down the sink." He had to pour it all out before they'd allow us to go back to our camp.

We got back into camp and everybody got straightened out. We had another week to go yet on our maneuvers. We had to lay a mine field. This took a few days. It was pretty touchy work. They weren't live explosives, but they were set with M-80s. If one of them went off, it could blow dirt in your eyes or really damage your thumbs and hands. We got finished with our maneuvers about a day early.

So our captain went in to the army base and he had some of the boys go with him. He bought a whole bunch of beer and ice. He had a "Beer Bust" for us. We had little assault boats as part of our equipment. We filled them full of ice and beer. We had a good time sitting around singing and telling stories. It was a great time to relax and have a good session with our officers. We all mingled together just like we were a family. I didn't know people could be so together—a group like that. That was one of the things I remember about Louisiana.

I guess we'd become a pretty good outfit. Some of the other outfits on the post respected ours because they thought of us as a "crack outfit." That's what they called us. We always met the challenge whenever there was a challenge of any kind.

After that, we started preparing to go overseas. We began getting leaves to go back home for the last time before we shipped out. I got to come home. That was hard for me because our house had burned. When I got the letter from my mom I was pretty sad. Some of my buddies came over to my bunk and they knew there was something wrong. They asked me what my problem was and so I told them. I let them read my letter. We used to do that a lot. Sometimes, if a certain person didn't get a letter, we just let them read ours. It would help. Some guys felt pretty bad if they didn't get a letter in the mail. My friends stood by me and helped me out in my sadness. Seems like there was always somebody with me every time I went anywhere. There were always three or four of us together. That's the way we were taught because we were having so many problems in the South. Even our captain who was from the South still made us buddy-up all the time to look out for one another.

When I went home, I come down the hill with my mother. I was driving the car. You have to come down a draw a ways and then you break out into a meadow and you can see where the house was. I come down the hill and down into the open and I had to stop. I couldn't hold my emotions. I cried. I was born in that house. The neighbor that lived across the draw let my mother and grandmother move into this other house because they weren't using that house anymore. They moved in, but they didn't have any clothing or anything. People gave them things. During the war, that was hard. Everything was so hard to come by, but they managed to get dishes, utensils, bedding, and things. So that's where my mother, my grandmother, and stepfather lived.

The fire happened in the morning. We never had an electric range so my stepdad built a hot fire in the kitchen stove. Then he went outside to do some things before he went to work. We had a stovepipe that come from the kitchen around through the one little bedroom and then into the chimney. I guess the stovepipe got pretty hot and it caught fire in the back room when my mother and grandmother were in the kitchen. By the time they noticed the fire, it was going pretty good. We never had any running water or faucets. The fire got away from them. They tried everything to get it out. It got so hot they couldn't even get close to it. My mother and grandmother just had to stand there and watch it burn. Neighbors came and tried to help. There wasn't any water close by or even a fire truck. We didn't have anything like that in our town. Our old fire department just had a bunch of hoses hooked onto a little cart with big wheels and that was our fire department. All the things we had burned. The things Grandma kept as keepsakes from her children, pictures, all my things, burned. Some of the buckskin dresses my grandaunt had there. Indian saddles, buffalo hides, our hair-braided bridles, old, old blankets—a lot of valuable things. Just one big, hot fire.

It took me about two days before I even would go across the draw and look at it. But I go there today. I can still visualize the house, the porch, everything in there just like it was. I still tell my wife every once in a while, "I'm getting homesick. I think I'll go home for a while." I'll go up there and spend a day by myself, walk

My father and mother, William Whitman Axtell and Nellie Moody in their 1923 wedding photo. (Axtell Family Archive).

Me, at the age of one. (Axtell Family Archive).

In 1945, I went back home for a visit.
Standing to my right is my maternal grand-
mother Jane Moody (74), and to my left is
her friend, Mary Oatman (age unknown).
(Axtell Family Archive)

Above,
my father, William
Whitman Axtell, at
forty-three, in his WWII
Air Force Aviation
Engineers uniform.
(Axtell Family Archive)
Above right,
my mother, Nellie
Moody, at 43.
(Axtell Family Archive)

The first photograph
I sent to my mother; I
was eighteen.
(Axtell Family Archive)

1991 publication of Way Out in Idaho:
A Celebration of Songs and Stories,
compiled by Rosalie Sorrels.
(Photo courtesy of Michael Cordell)

Working at Potlatch Corporation from 1951–1986.
(Axtell Family Archive)

*October 1994, Memorial Ceremony at the
Bear Paw Battlefield in Montana.
(Photo courtesy of Stan Hoggatt)*

Bottom, *Non-treaty Nez Perce — photo taken at
Spalding, Idaho, circa 1876. My paternal great-
grandfather* Timlpusmin *is standing second from
the right.*
*(Photo courtesy of Nez Perce National Historical
Park, Spalding, Idaho)*

Right,
*My war dance outfit.
(Photo courtesy of Ben
Marra Studios)*

"Dancing" — Genesee, Idaho, circa 1915,
photographer unknown.
(Photo courtesy of Nez Perce National
Historical Park, Spalding, Idaho)

around and visit the old foundation. I go up and visit my rock. To me it feels like I go home. I still think of that old place as my home.

My furlough, a fourteen-day leave, was mostly spent traveling on a train. Don't seem like you really enjoy your time home. You always try to do so many things in just a few days—go see a certain amount of people and try to explain to them that you are becoming a different person. You start to understand what war is all about and you start feeling what our old warriors went through back in the old times. I guess you could say it was in our blood—being a descendant of a warrior that died in a war. All the warriors that fought, all the ones that I talked to and I knew, how they told me to be brave—all these things were coming into place.

In my younger days, the old warriors would talk and I could listen to them tell stories around the woodstove. They'd tell stories after supper or dinner. We'd sit around before it was time to go to the sweat house, or in the evening after supper, before it was time to go to bed. Sometimes they wouldn't talk about war. Sometimes they'd talk about other things. Hunting or fishing. They were always good stories. Once in a while they'd get into spiritual things. It wasn't always just one subject.

I got strong instructions and good words from this warrior, Arthur Simon. He was a blind man then. I remember him telling stories to me about my great-grandfather who died in the war and how important a man he was. But the warriors never would tell each other about their powers, the powers they had. It wasn't anything that they would tell stories about. They all knew each other had a power of some kind, but they wouldn't come out and discuss it. When things are important to a certain person, like powers, they won't hardly reveal their stories. They would hand down some wisdom, some important instructions. This is what I experienced when I was getting ready to leave for the service. People would tell me about bravery and how to be strong, how to follow the footsteps of your ancestors and not be afraid or turn your back against your own people or your own soldiers.

I heard some stories about our own old people that turned against their own people—their own Nez Perce people here—by becoming scouts for the army and becoming informers and all kinds of things like that. The old warriors I knew were so against that because what them people did caused a lot of our people to die. That was a sad thing to hear, them stories like that about some of our own people turning and becoming scouts and informers. I don't like to talk about these people that betrayed their own people because it's sad. If my ancestors did that I wouldn't ever try to cover up for them in any way. I wouldn't try to put other people down that were brave and strong and had powers. I would be ashamed. But that has happened and hopefully will never happen again.

I tried to visit with all these important people who gave me these kinds of words and instructions. Up to this day I'm really happy that I knew my language and I could understand, because all these stories were told in *Nimiiputimpt*, our native Nez Perce language.

There's so many things that our old people knew about patience. I think that's where I got the patience to do a lot of things. Like my grandmother making gloves. She wouldn't hurry and sew. You know when you hurry and get behind, you sew fast. She wouldn't. She sewed that one way all the time. Same way with my mother

when she done her beadwork or making cornhusk bags.
It just took a long time. Patience.

When I would leave, my mom would never shed
tears. She would always smile and tell me to be careful.
I guess after I left she would cry. Big band music was
the thing in them days. I like music. I even tried to
learn to play an instrument one time. Mom could play
the piano. A lot of the old guys used to come and ask
her to chord for them when they had country dances.
My favorite bands were Benny Goodman, Artie Shaw,
Glenn Miller, and Tommy Dorsey. I try to collect all
those old performers because they had a lot to do with
the war effort. In high school I began listening to all
these different big bands. I got to know what time they
come on the radio in the evening. They all had different
programs to broadcast for the men that were already in
the service. I listened to these every time one of them
come on. Out where we lived we didn't have any electricity. We used to have to buy these little battery packs
to put in our radios. At certain times I wouldn't turn the
radio on because I wanted to save my battery for other
music and story programs my mother listened to. I
would never miss Glenn Miller when he got his band the
way he wanted it. He always had a fifteen-minute program sponsored by Chesterfied cigarettes. He had this
theme song, "Moonlight Serenade." I would never miss
that. I found out later that my mother got the habit of
listening to that after I was gone. Each time they would
play "Moonlight Serenade" it made her cry. I didn't
know that till later, after she had passed away.
Sometimes I listen to that now and I get that same feeling that, I guess, my mom did and it makes me lonely.
See, I was her only child and she would listen to that

every night. She was a very good mother. She always made sure that our radio was in working order so that I could listen to the big bands.

At camp we had stacks of records that were donated to our day room. We could go and listen to records, play pool, ping-pong, whatever. Some of the guys would play a certain song and you could see them get emotional also. We got to the point where we knew each other's favorite songs. We'd go to the PX and say, "I'll play a certain song for my friend." We knew that he had a connection to home with that certain song.

That's the way I felt. Every time I would hear this "Moonlight Serenade" someplace I could connect myself to the old house and my little, old radio I had. It would just bring me right to the living room. That's the way I think a lot of the music was to us. It was a very important part of being away from home and being in the war. I'd hear some trumpeter like Harry James and it reminded me of a man that was our role model up there at Ferdinand. His name was Alvin. He used to come and stay at our house. In the evenings, he would get his trumpet out and play on our front porch and it would echo down the draw. It was just beautiful. Sometimes you could hear the neighbor's dogs howl way down over the hill.

I visited some cousins. I had dinner with them. After dinner I found out the kids had the mumps. I didn't think nothing of it till I got back to the base and found out I had them. We stopped at New Orleans, and the captain got permission to get us out on the platform to do calisthenics. We counted cadence while we were exercising. I guess we were at it for about ten minutes when we looked around and saw we had about a thousand spectators. They heard us and they came to watch us. Each time we'd finish an exercise these people would applaud. They were so enthused. We were in uniform, but we had our shirts off and white undershirts showing. After we seen all them people, everybody counted off really loud. As more people would come they'd holler, "More, more!" It was a morale builder. We had to get on the train and get ready to leave.

We stopped in another town. When we came to a stop, three little black boys come running down on the platform. They started to dance and all of us clapped. They were tap dancing and they were good. So we all threw money out there to them—nickels and dimes. When our train pulled out they were still dancing. All these guys from the other rail cars behind us went by and saw them. I wonder how much money them boys got. They were throwing dimes, quarters, nickels, whatever they had.

All along the way there were people who came by. Some of them would hand out cigarettes. It was just like that during the war—togetherness. I think our president we had at the time was pretty much a big part of this because of the way he handled the war. That was President Franklin D. Roosevelt. He had everybody thinking the same and everybody doing the same. To me, he was outstanding—a strong leader, especially with two wars going on at the same time. He brought the people together. Everybody was cooperating.

On the way to the Port of Embarkation in New York, I broke out with the mumps. I got a sore throat and couldn't hardly swallow. I said, "Oh, I guess I got it."

I was bunking with another friend from Craigmont, Idaho. He was non-Indian. I infected him also. So they took both of us off the train when we got to New York and took us to the hospital. That's where I parted company with my outfit, the 529th Engineers, the Light Pont and Bridge Company. We were going to go to Europe. I had made it that far with that outfit and it was pretty hard for me to get left behind. I had a good position there. I was motor pool dispatcher. I got to know my job and work. I done a lot to get our equipment on the proper places on the box cars and on the train. It was sad to lay in the hospital and wonder where they were at and what they were doing. After the war was over, I ran into some of them. We had a lot of experiences to exchange.

After I got out of the hospital, they took me over to a replacement center near New Brunswick, New Jersey. They wouldn't allow you to catch another ship or anything like that. There was no way to fly so we were just left behind. We didn't have air travel like we do nowadays. I didn't realize there were so many people that had the same problems at this replacement center—got left behind for some reason or were just there. We had about four or five double barracks full of people. Once in a while an outfit would come by shipping out and they needed so many replacements because some of them didn't pass the physicals and they'd take some soldiers with them. They'd put us on alert and we couldn't leave the camp or our barracks. I always tried to get in some way, but I never did get picked to go. I always wanted to go to Europe where my outfit was. I hoped there was some way I could get back to them, but it never did work out. I was there about two months.

It was July 1944 at the replacement center. We did a lot of calisthenics and close-order drills, but most of the time it was all recreation—volleyball, baseball, softball, horseshoes, you name it. That's what we had to do all day to keep ourselves occupied. Never had any training classes of any kind while we were there. I had guard duty about once a month. I went to New York a few times. Sometimes we went on pass to New Brunswick. On the Fourth of July, they told us there was going to be a big military competition at Rutgers Stadium. People from all different outfits would be there so they got a bunch of us together that could march and drill real good. We didn't have any rifles or anything like that. We formed a platoon and drilled everyday. We thought we were pretty good.

On the day of the competition we got out there and done our thing. After we got through we run up to the stands to watch the rest of them. Then this MP outfit got out there—the black MPs. Talk about good. We didn't even come close to them guys. They didn't even have a guy shouting commands. They did it all by the numbers and in their minds. Everything was perfect. They had good equipment, too. They had white leggings and white cartridge belts and white gloves. They looked sharp.

One day they cleared out that area and sent us to Pennsylvania. They separated out the Air Force and the different branches. I got sent to Camp Reynolds, Pennsylvania. It was another replacement center, similar to the one we had just left. I was there another two months. During that time, we had to dress parade on Saturdays. A band would come out and play and we would have to march and dress parade in front of the general of the camp. They gave us a little training there. A little bit, not that much. We had to do a lot of drilling and it was getting old by then. Pretty boring. I always thought about going back to my outfit. I still had my two stripes, but I got to the point where I took them off. I just wanted to be a soldier.

We must've been there about a month when we got a call from Philadelphia that there was a riot there. People were jumping on these street cars and motor coaches, robbing, and it was getting out of hand. They made a kind of regiment out of us and took us over there. We stayed about three weeks. The first two weeks, we rode the street cars armed with rifles till it died down. All that time we didn't have any pay. All of us were broke, penniless in this big city. Of course we could ride all the street cars we wanted 'cause it was free. We were also based next to a big amusement park. We could go in and ride anything we wanted just for the fun. A lot of the guys were bored with that after a while.

We got to go to different recreational things and I liked to go to the baseball games. We'd either watch the Philadelphia Athletics or the Philadelphia Phillies. We didn't have all the top athletes at the time because most of them were in the service. But it was still good to go see a big-league ball game. The sad part of it was we'd have to sit so far up in the bleachers where we couldn't hardly see the ball. When they'd throw the ball from the pitcher to the catcher, you couldn't see the motion. At home I used to listen to them on the radio. I used to listen to the World Series.

It was a real good experience to be in such a big city. To bring peace in the town and community. We did our job. People were so kind to us. We never had a payday all that time and they gave us cigarettes and all kinds of things. It was a lot different than being in the South. There was quite a difference in the North and the South back then.

We went back to camp and one day they put us on alert. That was something I had been hoping for—not that I wanted to leave Pennsylvania. That was one of the best places I've ever been in. The people were so good to us. We used to walk in the streets and they'd give us personal invitations to "come and eat dinner" or "come and eat breakfast" or "come and eat supper." We could go from one church to another and eat and have a good time. Lots of families would take us out to little barbecues. We got to meet so many people. It was probably the friendliest place I've ever been to. There was a little place where you could wait, like a bus stop. Instead of using it for a bus stop, we'd stand there and people driving into town would stop and we'd hitch rides. We didn't even have to thumb. A car would stop and several of us would jump in and they'd say, "Oh, we can take three of you guys." And three of us would jump in and we would go. It wasn't a bus stop, it was a hitchhiker post. Each time a car would stop, so many guys would get in and away they'd go. If there was only room for one guy in the car, we'd holler back, "Room for one!" and then one guy would come up and get in. That's the way it was. We always got into town for free. Once in a while you'd have to catch the bus back, but not very often. I kind of hated to leave that camp.

Then we got the word. They told us to pack up. They called our names out. They started with the As: Adams, Anderson, and all the others. I crossed my fingers and they hollered my name, "Axtell!" Oh boy, I was going to leave! We got all ready and they marched us out to a holding area. We stood around for a couple of hours and waited for the trucks to bring us into the railroad station. Nobody knew where we were going. They wouldn't tell us. We had two or three staging areas. They separated us. Some guys were going one place and we were going some other place. Finally we got our trucks. We hopped on and they took us in.

We got on railroad cars. We said, "We must not be going very far." We didn't have Pullman cars. Usually they gave us Pullman cars if we were going to take a long ride. It was a long ride and we had to sit up most of the way. That was terrible. After we boarded, this chubby, little captain came through. He was our train commander. After we got rolling he told us we were going to a camp in Alabama. He said, "There's another holding place there, a replacement area." More softball, more volleyball. It wasn't much to look forward to.

When we got to Pittsburgh and the steel mills, we stopped. We were getting ready to pull out and some-how the tracks got messed up or something. Anyway, a train backed into our train and derailed us. We didn't tip over, but it shook us up a little. We got knocked off the track. The captain had some paperwork to do, so he made us some passes to go into town while we waited for our car to be put back on the rails again. Of course, we didn't have any money. Seems like we were always behind a pay day here or there. Finally we got our train fixed and we headed out. The next morning we woke up and we were all dirty. Our clothes were all dirty from the steel mills. We didn't realize how much dust and stuff was in that town of Pittsburgh.

We were on the train all day and all night again. The next day we pulled into Alabama. The trucks were there to greet us and take us on into camp. It was the same procedure again. It was getting pretty tiresome by now. I didn't really care to be sent back to the South, to see the same thing over again. Alabama was a dry state at the time. That wasn't good news to some of our boys. That meant we had to stay in camp and go to the PX to get beer.

At the replacement center, it was the same thing

again: softball, volleyball, horseshoes. Those who didn't participate in sports had to drill. They found out I had stripes. They chose certain noncommissioned officers to give drills. I always like to talk strong. Whenever I'm asked to speak, I speak fairly loud. The men liked to have me do drills because they said they could hear me plain. After several days out there, I kept getting more people. That was kind of odd. They didn't want to play baseball, they wanted to come drill with me. Pretty soon I had a whole bunch of guys out there and we were having fun.

We were there about two weeks and we were still out of pay. This one guy went to the chaplain on post and told him what our problem was. So the chaplain got some money for him through the Red Cross or the Salvation Army. That night we had a nice time at the PX. He ended up with the name "Chaplain." He was buying and we all had a good time.

One afternoon they called a bunch of names again. They called my name and I ran up and packed my duffel bag. I went right out there on the street and waited. The sergeant was sent over to march us because we had to pack our own bags. They didn't bring the trucks over, so we had to shoulder these heavy bags. Right away we could see this sergeant was frustrated or something. But we had been pushed around so much, you know. We didn't react to his commands that fast. All of us were that way. He got mad at us and tried to make us march in step. He counted cadence. He wanted us to get in step and nobody would do it. He got pretty mad at us. He even gave us the command to double time, but nobody would do it. By the time we got to the company area, he was hotheaded. Luckily, I never got in his company.

I was put in the 1298th Combat Engineer Battalion, Company C. Our first sergeant was an Indian man from Oklahoma. He was an old army man with hash marks from his elbow to his wrist—about a thirty-year man. All kinds of ribbons on his chest and kind of a hefty guy. He never did acknowledge me as Native American. He never felt like he was a Native American to me. I guess he'd been in the army so long, maybe he forgot his heritage or his traditions. He acted like a white man to me. After I seen the way he was, I didn't bother with him. I just stayed out of his way.

By this time we found out we were going to have to take basic training all over again. This was a shocker. Most of us had already been through basic training and advanced training. There we were, just like a bunch of rookies. We started basic training right from scratch. Another thirteen weeks. We had to learn about hand-to-hand combat, everything that has to do with being a combat soldier. Some of the noncommissioned officers that we got had already been in combat. They were brought back from the European theater to train us to go to the South Pacific.

I became a squad leader and a ration truck driver for a while. I picked up the rations from the warehouse and distributed them to the different companies. I had an assistant, a different person every day. I had a good thing going there. Every morning we'd line up for work call and I wouldn't have to. I'd just report down to the motor pool and check out my truck and do my run. I was happy breaking away from all that basic training stuff. I was getting really accustomed to making my run and having a little free time where I could drive my truck down to the main post and to go the serviceman's club. Being a motor pool dispatcher, I could check out a few miles where I could fill it in with paper work. I went down to the cleaners and picked up uniforms for some of my friends. I done this for about three weeks.

One evening I was sitting at the barracks and a Charge of Quarters, a CQ, come by and hollered my name. I went down and he said, "You got an emergency phone call."

My stepdad called from home and told me my mother had cancer. She was getting very sick. He said they were going to do surgery on her. The commander let me go home. We finally got retroactive pay and I had some money. They took me into town and I got my tickets on the train. You know, you ride the train, it don't seem like it's going fast enough. You want to get there fast. It was such a long ride. You see a lot of different people. You got to make these different changes in the big city like Chicago. You come up with one railroad then you got to go clear across town to Grand Central Station to catch a train going west. Servicemen had priorities, but servicemen and their wives got to be the first ones on the cars. I was waiting my turn there when this one young lady come up and said, "Can I be your wife for a while?" She was in a hurry and she wanted to get through.

I said, "I guess so."

She hung on to me and we went through the line together. I didn't know who she was, but I guess she had done a lot of traveling already like that. She was nice. I got her through and I never did see her again.

After changing in Chicago, I got into Spokane, Washington, late at night. The bus from Spokane to Lewiston left the bus station at five o'clock in the morning. The next morning when I got to Lewiston, my stepdad was waiting there with a little pickup. He was a person who could get a job real easy and he was working in the hospital while my mother was in there. I told him I was pretty well beat and went to his room and laid down and slept quite a while.

He come and told me, "Your mother is wanting to see you real bad."

I cleaned up and I went over to the hospital. She was so happy to see me. That was the first time I ever seen her shed tears like that.

She said, "Oh, I had to get sick. I didn't want to get sick, but I guess I had to."

That afternoon they went and done surgery. I stayed with her for three days until she recovered from the operation. She was asleep for a long time. When she woke up she seen me sitting there.

"You been sitting there all this time?"

I said, "Yeah. I was waiting for you to wake up."

"Oh," she said. "I'm glad. I was dreaming. I dreamed you was already gone."

I said, "No. I got a few days left."

She went to sleep and I walked downtown, had dinner, and went to a movie. After the movie I went back to the hospital. I could tell she was getting weak. I wired and asked for an extension of my emergency leave. The colonel wired back and said to take seven more days. She started getting better, becoming herself again.

I said, "I can go back I guess, Mom?"

She said, "Yeah. You can go back now. I think I'm going to be alright."

I think I made her sad in a way because I met this one woman. She was a little older than me and already had a child. My mother didn't want me to get involved with her, but she wouldn't come out and tell me. She said, "Just don't get yourself tied down. You're still young. It was hard for me to say, "I'm going now." When someone is not well, it's hard to walk away. Especially when you don't know if you're ever coming back again. My new orders told me to report to Camp Shelby, Mississippi. I didn't know at the time that the woman I was chasing around with was pregnant. People think she tricked me into marrying her. I don't know, but it seems that way now when I think about it. It was war time and I guess I needed company pretty badly.

I was in Mississippi for about two months when I got a phone call again. My mother had passed on.

I told my captain, "I don't have any money."

He made a few phone calls and said, "The Red Cross is willing to loan you money but you have to sign some kind of agreement."

He said he'd try the Salvation Army. They said, "Give us his name and address, where's he going, and we'll have the tickets ready for him." Just like that.

I asked the captain, "When do they want to get paid back?"

He said, "That's not necessary. If you can pay them back, that's fine. But if you can't, you don't have to."

The captain had one of his chief drivers take me into town. We used to call him "Shoulder Holster." He felt sad for me, I guess, because I was going home to bury my mother. He said, "I got a couple dollars here in my pocket. You can have it."

We were all broke, but my other friends scraped up a few bucks for me. It didn't last me very long because I had a long journey. When I got a couple days out, I was broke. I spent that money for something to eat. When I got to Chicago I was pretty flat. I had an eight-hour lay-over there. Eight hours seems like a long time when you have to lay over. To pass the time away I went and walked to this big servicemen's center on the way to the

Grand Central Station. I was getting to know Chicago pretty good by then.

They had all kinds of food there. You could eat just about anything you wanted. I sat down and had me lots to eat. The center had different levels. The bottom level had all the food. The second level was a recreation room where they had sofas and chairs to sit on and reading places. In the next room they had pool tables, and ping-pong tables, and records. On the top floor they had sleeping bunks. You could go up there and sleep if you wanted. I got through eating and I went up to the second level and I sat in one of the big chairs for a while.

Someone hollered out, "Anybody who wants to go to the hockey game can come up here and get a ticket." It sounded like a good idea. I went and got a ticket. Didn't know nothing about a hockey game. There's so much to see in a live hockey game. You just follow the puck around and wherever it goes, that's where the action is. You just sit there with your mouth open, watching how in the heck can they move around like that in them skates?

I went back to the servicemen's center after the game and got talking with this lady at the desk. I asked her if there was anything else I could go to or see. "I got six more hours here to kill."

She said, "Why don't you go across the street here? There's a Museum of Natural History over there. Servicemen can go in free."

I had to keep myself occupied. I spent the rest of my time over there. I found a Nez Perce display and that brought me so close to home. I seen all these little statues. They had them dressed in our own Indian regalia and a lot of our different things. They showed people working on buckskin and making hides. I spent my time in just that one area where the Nez Perce part of it was. I walked out and I was feeling pretty good.

Before I left Chicago, I got me a little bag and I poked some sandwiches in there and some oranges, pieces of cupcakes, cookies. About the second day from Chicago, I run out. I didn't have anymore. Every time the train would stop for a station I'd jump off and see if I could find a Salvation Army or Red Cross stand and get some stuff.

Early in the morning we come past Havre, Montana. It was January. Boy, was it cold, really cold. I was going to jump off and I seen how cold it was, so I got back on and I sat there in my seat. This one lady was sitting there facing me. I wouldn't say she was old, but she was probably in her fifties. She seen me getting back on and I didn't have no lunch or box or anything. She come over and sat by me.

She said, "I've been watching you. You jump off and get stuff to eat. Where are you headed?"

I told her I was going to Lewiston, Idaho, and I lived not too far from there. My mother had passed away and I was going home. I told her I was running a little short of funds so that's why I would jump off and grab me some cold sandwiches.

She said, "I have three boys in the service." She told me where they were. One was in the navy and the other two were in the army.

She said, "You come with me because today, this morning, you're going to have a good breakfast."

She took me into the diner and I had some ham and eggs, toast, hashbrowns. Boy, did I have a good meal. Breakfast is my favorite meal anyway. She was real nice and paid my meal. She even gave me five dollars. I wish I could remember her name. These things stand out in your mind when you have a hard time. When we got to Spokane I got off the train and thanked that woman again. She told me to have a good visit at home "even though you're here for a sad reason." She told me to build up courage in myself.

It was cold. I went to the bus depot and the ticket was a little bit more than the five-dollar bill in my pocket. I couldn't get on. So I said, "Well, I guess I got to hitch. That's the only way I'm going to get home."

So I got up and walked out of Spokane. That was cold. Really cold. Back in the old days there weren't all them freeways there. You had to walk out and hit that main road coming down. Traffic was very, very slow because it was war time. I seen a truck with stock racks coming. I stuck out my thumb and he stopped. He was an old guy.

He said, "I'll give you a ride, but it's gonna be a cold one. My heater don't work and my window's busted off on top."

I mean, it was cold. He had an old quilt there and he told me to cover up and I did.

He said, "I'm going as far as Colfax."

He had to pick up some cattle or something. He had an old Chevrolet truck. I could feel myself shivering, but I had a ride.

When we got to Colfax he said, "Right over there is a coffee shop."

He gave me a dollar bill and told me to go get some coffee. Now I had six dollars. I got some coffee and a sandwich. I sat in there maybe forty-five minutes and got myself warmed up. I got back on the road again and walked clear up to the top of the hill where you come around this curve. Here come a car. I set my bag down and stuck out my thumb. This old Ford car stopped. It was a man and his wife.

He said, "Where you going soldier?"

I said, "I'm going to Lewiston."

He said, "That's where we're going. My wife and I, we're going there to see the doctor." They had a heater in their little car and I got in the back. It was a nice ride.

I got to Lewiston and called Ferdinand where my aunt was. She didn't have a phone in the house, but the guy that run the central office would go and deliver a message for a dollar. So I told him to go and tell my aunt and my family that I was in Lewiston. She called me back and told me that somebody had come down to meet Leander, my cousin. He was in the navy and came home for the funeral, too. He was married. He and his wife had one little baby already. My stepdad came down with that little pickup again and they rode in front and I ended up riding in the back. Boy, was it cold. My stepdad brought a whole bunch of quilts and blankets down and I covered up. I lay in the back and rode home like that. Finally we got home.

I went inside and Grandma was sitting in there. We greeted each other, then we sat there and both cried. All that time we lived together, my mother, my grandmother, and I, we never thought a thing like this was going to happen.

She said, "Well, let's go over. I want you to see her. What kind of clothes do you want her to have? What casket do you want her to be in?"

They had her in a mortuary over in Craigmont. My stepdad wanted me to be the one to pick out the things. I had to make the funeral arrangements and find out who was available for pallbearers and to be the preacher.

It was about twenty below zero at Ferdinand. Some men came up from Kamiah. They dug Mom's grave. I went out there and seen where the grave was. They were all bundled up and taking turns digging. It was hard digging when it was cold. The Seventh-Day Adventist Church let us keep my mother's body in state over there and the townspeople came to view the body. Different people gave prayers. The priest came over and had a rosary for her because she was a member of the community. The Indian Presbyterian Church came out and had prayers the night before the funeral.

The funeral was at the little church in Meadow Creek, at Ferdinand. It was the Indian Presbyterian Church. It was so cold we couldn't get from the gate to the church. They had to bring the hearse to the gate and then they had to carry the body from there to the church. People came all bundled up in woolen clothes. It was awful cold. It was crowded in the church and people had to stand outside. I know it was very uncomfortable for a lot of people, but they still went. One man sang a solo in memory of my mother. I was good friends with the girl who played the piano for him. After the service was all over we went back to Ferdinand.

I was sitting with Grandma. We were talking and visiting with my cousins and other close relations. Somebody answered a knock at the door. The man who was in charge of the grange was there and I told him to come on in. I was a member of the grange, too. All the servicemen became members.

He said, "We just took up a collection for you. We come up with $150.00."

They had announced at the church that I came home on leave and I was short-funded. It was something that I wasn't expecting. I got emotional. I felt like I was really home. That this was where my life was and that was why I was representing this town, defending this country. A lot of things came to mind. I guess people appreciated my mother because she played piano for the grange and all their dances. She became well-respected. I was a part of that. I had so much to think about in just that little instance.

The Presbyterian Church in Kamiah, called "The Second Church," put on a benefit dinner for me. They raised about a hundred dollars also. I had money to help pay for the funeral expense. I didn't want to take it all back with me because I knew my life was going to be different. I knew it was going to be hard and I was probably going to do some things I'd regret. I felt like part of my body was gone. I knew things were not going to work out in the direction I was going. Things materialized in my mind that I wasn't going to be the same. I just had that feeling and that's the way it turned out.

I started to drink and do other things. I became very irritable. I couldn't get along with some people and I let them know in a way you're not supposed to. I kept getting involved in fights. I was changing. I couldn't realize I was taking out all my frustrations on my friends. I wasn't the soldier I was before. I neglected my duties. I just couldn't pull it together again.

I went on this way for a while. It was hard to wake up in the morning. My first thought used to be, "I wonder how Mom is?" To wake up after she died, I'd think, "Mom's not here." Then I started thinking about my grandma. My aunt wrote me a real nice letter telling me about things that people said and how my grandmother was handling herself after losing her oldest daughter. I came back to reality again. My mom wouldn't be very proud of me like this. She was proud of me before she died. I thought about the music that connected me with her.

I started pulling myself out of it, slowly. It took about seven months. I went back to being a squad leader again. I picked myself up. I went to the PX and had a good time. I started getting along with my friends. I apologized.

They said, "We understand how things are. We all like you."

One of the boys in the squad we named "Deacon." When we had money we'd go to the PX and have our good time on Saturday or on any other night. We'd all get to feeling pretty good and then we'd come back to the barracks. We'd say, "Well, Deacon. Give us a sermon."

We'd stack up three foot lockers and he'd get the soldier's handbook out and lay it in front. Then he'd give us a sermon. This got to be a ritual. Every time we'd come back we'd stack our foot lockers and he'd preach to us. He could really carry on, just like he was a preacher. He'd get to rolling pretty good sometimes, you know, Southern Baptist style. It seemed like the more we done that, the better he got.

When it was about time for us to get ready and ship out, we went to the PX one night. We were about three men short in our squad. Some of our boys couldn't pass the physical so they got shipped out and we got three young replacements. When we come back from the PX they were already in bed. So we stacked up the lockers and old Deacon started preaching. Boy, he was preaching a hard sermon about preparing people to go to war. Oh, he had it all down pat. These three young boys were pretty scared, I guess. They came forward. He converted them.

He looked over at me and said, "Chief, what the hell am I going to do now?"

I said, "I don't know. You're the preacher."

He said, "What if I have to baptize them?"

"Well, that's up to you," I said.

He didn't know what to do. He got himself off the hook somehow. He was decent enough to take them three boys to the Chaplain. Even though he was kind of drunk when he done all this, he put it in the right perspective and I really admire him for that. Deacon.

People were going home on leave for the last time. That's when I found out I was going to be a father. I didn't know how to deal with this because I didn't have a mom to go to. No one to ask. So I dealt with it in a difficult way. It wasn't working out the way a relationship should. I knew it wasn't going to work. I had that feeling. I tried to do my best with it. I went to visit people who said encouraging things before I left the first time.

Everything was a little bit wilder for me. I was doing things. I wasn't staying home like I did when my mother was alive. I didn't care about staying at Ferdinand because I felt so lonely up there. I just chased around from Lapwai to Kamiah and all around—partying most of the time.

I went back to camp and waited for our time to ship out. It seemed like I didn't even care anymore. I found out we were going to the South Pacific. The time came and we had to catch the train. Instead of going to New York like we did the other time, we went west. It was the same pattern I used when I went home. Just after I got through going out, I went back. It's always different traveling on a troop train than it is on a passenger train. They gave us Pullman cars so we could have a place to sleep. It was a big train. We had four different companies and a battalion. That's a lot of men. I guess they kept us more confined for that reason. They were probably afraid of some of us going over the hill. It was a different time.

It was hard for people to go through their home towns. Going through their backyards, you might say, on their way to the Pacific. We went close by their homes and you'd see the sadness in the person's face and the tears in his eyes. We come through the Plains and I saw some of the places where Indian people lived. In my own way of thinking I can always tell when I'm close to an Indian village. You see a bunch of old cars with a trunk and windows open. Seems to me we Indian people always have a bunch of old cars and dogs around.

We come through North Dakota and through the upper part of Montana. I looked out the window and seen two Indian people riding a horse. That made me sad. I had to leave my horse when I left home. I worked for a man and helped him drive his cattle from one pasture to another. He used to watch my horse work with the cattle.

He said, "When you go to the service what are you going to do with your horse?"

I said, "I don't know. I guess I'll have to sell him."

He said, "I'll buy him."

He was a good horse. He once belonged to *Wetescickanin*, Earth Blanket (Covered With An Earth Blanket). I was in high school when *Wetescickanin* visited us one day. He was a big man and I nicknamed him "Jumbo." He was blind in his right eye and always wore a bandana over it. My mother looked out the window, down the canyon, and said, "There comes *Wetescickanin* and he's walking. He's leading his horse and he's coming really slow."

Grandma said, "Go open the gate."

I ran across the draw and when he got there I opened the gate. I asked him what happened.

He told me, "I think maybe it was a snake. It scared my horse and he jumped and I fell off. I lay there a long time. The horse didn't leave me. I finally got on the horse and when we come down here it started hurting real bad. That's when I started to walk."

He went on into the house and laid there, moaning and groaning, for several days. Grandma told me what to do to take good care of him. Finally, about the fourth or fifth day, he started eating a little soup and bread.

"It hurts right here," he said pointing to his abdomen.

I think he might have cracked a rib or something. Grandma took a sheet and made him a kind of brace or belt and tied it around him. He said he felt better. He started coming to the table, sitting in a chair. He was still walking pretty slow.

One morning he said, "Catch my horse."

I said to myself, "He can hardly walk good, yet, and he wants the horse."

I went out, got him, and brushed him off. I saddled him up and rode him around a bit, then tied him up around a post.

I told *Wetescickanin*, "The horse is all ready."

He got up and slowly went outside. The horse whinnied. It was glad to see him. He talked to his horse, petted him, walked around, looked at the saddle and pulled it back and forth.

I wondered, "What's he doing anyway?

He got all through and went over and took the reins off the post and said, "Where are you?"

"Back here."

He took the reins and gave them to me.

"He's yours."

He told Grandma, "This boy helped heal me."

He gave me that horse, the saddle, and the bridle. I ran upstairs to my room and grabbed my hat and coat. I ran back down, got on the horse and was gone for two days.

He was well trained. When I opened a gate he'd come through, turn around and face me. I wouldn't have to take the reins off. There were so many little things he used to do for me that just come natural. I got so attached to him.

So I felt really sad when I looked out and seen these two Indian boys riding. It took me right back to home. There's so many things to see along the way. You look around and you don't know whether you're going to be able to come back and see these things again. You don't know. This is the way it was.

We come through Spokane—just a few miles away, you might say. I looked this way to see, to look. That's what our old Indian people taught me. Even if you can't see what you want to see, you still look in that direction. So that's what I did. In my mind I could see the river here, and the road going up from the Camas Prairie to where I used to live. It was hard to go through Spokane like that. We went on into the Tri-Cities, Washington, area. All the way down the Columbia River and right by Celilo. There were no dams then. I could see Indian people out there walking around, building their scaffolds, getting ready for the fall fishing season. This was in late June or early July. We stopped at The Dalles, Oregon, and everybody looked out the window and hollered at people, saying "hi."

A couple friends of mine looked out the window and said, "Hey, there's an Indian girl out there."

I poked my head out the window and hollered. I kept hollering until she seen me. I called her over. She was awful shy and didn't want to say anything. I think she was standing there waiting for somebody. I told her that I was a Nez Perce from Lewiston, Idaho. She responded a little bit then.

I said, "I'm on my way overseas and I don't know where I'm going. We're just stopping here for a little bit." I told her to say hi to certain people, but she didn't even know who I was talking about.

We went to Portland and got off the train. The trucks met us and hauled us across the river to a place called Vancouver Barracks. While we were there we had to take shots. It seemed like every time we turned around we were getting more shots of some kind. Then we got quarantined. They wouldn't let us go nowhere for three or four days. On the fourth day, they finally allowed us to have a twelve-hour pass to town. My buddy and I took off and went to Portland to a movie. After the movie we went to a burlesque show. It was an old, raggedy place. We were sitting there watching and all of a sudden we seen a rat running around down below us. It wasn't that great a show anyway.

We left and found a nice tavern. We met some people there and they invited us out to a place called Vamport. It was a big housing project close to the river, west of Portland. It was for all the defense workers in Vamport City. When everybody started going to sleep, we had to go back. We hailed a cab. He stopped and we jumped in the back. We didn't have any money. As soon as he stopped at the barracks we jumped out and both run in different directions. I don't know if you call that an Indian trick or not, but it worked. He stood there hollering and we jumped the fence. It was already seven in the morning and our comrades were packed and waiting for the trucks to come. Boy, we changed in a hurry. Our buddies helped us pack our bags. As we got finished the trucks came. We moved out.

The journey to Hawaii took about fourteen days. Everybody got seasick. You had to wear a lifejacket all the time. We had to change direction every so often because of torpedoes. That was for our protection. It was kind of scary. They woke us up one morning and all the things we heard about on the radio and seen on the movies was there. You just stand there and try to imagine in your own mind how the Japanese came. We got to go to Scofield Barracks.

We laid around in Hawaii. They gave us the word and we saddled up again. It was a long ride from there to Japan. That's when we found out we were going there. We were a large fleet of ships. That gave us orientation. It was a long, long ride — something like twenty-eight days. The bomb had already dropped. The buildings in Nagasaki were torn apart, just like something got inside and pushed out. That's the way they all looked — scattered outward. Along the waterfront where all these plants were, they were all destroyed. It was an awful sight to see. So much destruction this one bomb did. Little kids running around. A school on the hill never got touched — that's what we used for our barracks. We fixed it and set up our own area. We had our own electricity. After things got settled down, we started hiring Japanese workers.

When we went into Nagasaki, we had to take some money. We had to take our boots off outside of this little place. We had some Japanese food there. They served us sake. When we come back outside some wise guy went and scattered all the boots. We sat around for quite a while before we had our own boots.

The children began to mean a lot to me. We'd go eat our chow in the mess hall. The first time I went to dump my garbage, all these little hands come out toward me. They were scared to do that with the other soldiers. They'd push them aside, cuss at them. So I started putting bread in my jacket. It was easy for me. I felt a little different about the children, because now I had one of my own. It took a while for the letters to get to me that I had a son. I wrote back and said I wanted to have either his first or middle name be William, after my father. The message got through because his name is Charles William Axtell and he was born in 1945. So the little ones that were eating off of my mess gear, after I got finished eating my own dinner, were more special to me. But the other soldiers still mistreated these little ones. It was different for me because they all liked me. It was just like being a part of them.

But I always thought to myself, "What if this would've happened the other way around? What if these little ones here were some of my cousins or relatives at home? Being hungry like this?"

I have a different way of looking at things. All my life I've been that way. I guess it's because I was the only child my mother had and I always wanted to find relations or close friends all the time. I think being Indian, growing up the way I did, and seeing the way the old people would come and live with one another and take care of one another for long periods of time, was a teaching for me. There was so much love exchanged. It was just a relationship that they developed all the time. I seen all these things and it was a wonderful teaching. I still have the same thoughts today as to how we should feel toward one another. That goes for all people—all races.

I helped the young ones over there in my own way. I didn't make a big deal of it, but I was sneaking around helping them and feeling sorry for them because some of them were homeless.

I seen a lot of things happen in Japan. A Japanese man didn't understand what an American officer was trying to tell him. So this officer just kicked him around. I couldn't say nothing, because this man was an officer. You just stood there and watched. It sure didn't make me feel very good to see all these things happen. The war was over. The treaty was signed. Then again, to me, treaty is just a word. It brought feelings back to me, especially since I am a Nez Perce Indian.

No matter what happens, we make treaties and still "the treatment" goes on. They should have called it "treatments" instead of "treaties." That's the way I look at it, because, even today, our treaties aren't being lived up to. In these modern times, I imagine the treaties have changed with the Japanese people. Look how much they have accomplished and look how much the Indians have accomplished. We're still in a rut. You can see how much more treaties mean in foreign countries. Even over in Germany, their treaties are probably more lived up to than they are here. We're still here and we're still fighting these treaties.

Why should that happen?

Maybe someday somebody will explain this to me. You might say we are being kicked around just like that Japanese man. Maybe not physically, but there never seems to be any real truce. The promises are not being lived up to with the Indian people here in the United States or in Canada.

Both sides, the American and the Japanese, had to give in and let bygones be bygones. I realize that there were a lot of brothers, cousins, fathers, and relations that got killed. It caused bitter feelings. I, too, lost close friends and some relations. But you have to be glad that it's over so that there will be no more killing like that.

One day my friend and first sergeant says to me, "Axtell, you're going home. I just got the call. Looks like you're about ready to head back."

From Fukuoka, to Nagoya, and then to Hiroshima. We got off the train and they took us across town. Oh jeez, it was just a mass of rubble. The whole thing was flat. Nothing was standing. It was all just a mass of rubble. I took the little boy I'd been looking after and told my first sergeant, "This is the little guy I've been helping. Look after him for me." He was crying and I had to leave him. Sometimes I wonder about him.

We loaded up on a big victory ship, went up on deck, and looked back to see Japan for the last time. Nobody waved good-bye to us or anything. We just left. On the ship is when I actually seen people integrated. The black people were along with us in the ship and bunking inside and nobody said anything about it.

Everybody had some kind of plan, what they were going to do, who they were going to call first when they got to the States. You don't realize things are going to happen that quickly. Being in the service so long we thought, "Well, this is going to be a long process." Actually, they pushed us right through.

We didn't log them days at sea, even though a big storm come up for about three days. It was scary.

People were sick. And what do you think they had for chow? Boiled eggs. And boiled eggs was running all over the place, rolling around. During the storm they radioed back to us that the ship ahead of us lost some men off the side, we weren't even allowed to go look out. We were supposed to have gone from Nagoya straight over to Seattle. Instead we had to drift further south to San Francisco.

They kept telling us, "We're getting closer to San Francisco." Nobody was going down to the bunks. Everybody stayed up on deck.

Somebody said, "Hey, we see lights."

It must've been 10:00 at night. The sky was lit up. San Francisco. Everybody was happy and kind of sad because our close buddies weren't coming back. At exactly midnight, we come underneath the Golden Gate Bridge. You could look up and see the cars going across the bridge. We anchored between Alcatraz and Fisherman's Wharf. I don't think anybody slept that night.

People used to call us the Nez Perce Nation, but I like Nez Perce Tribe better. That makes a distinction. I live in Idaho. That's another distinction. I live in America. I think I like that better than United States. It explains itself better. How can we call ourselves "United States" when each state has its own little government? I think most of us understand how valuable our own land and our own country are. The veterans of the wars that had to suffer and leave their homeland to do wars under-stand.

But the meaning of being united is something else to think about. I don't think it means that we should forget our own ways or our own language. Even though the word says we're united, it's only to a certain extent we're united. We're of a different color, a different race, and a different breed. And we can't ever, ever get away from that. The word "united" is very strong, but even today we see we're not. Our government especially. I don't see how we can classify ourselves as being united. I'm not criticizing my country, but there are a lot of things I see happening. One party of our government will get into office and the other party that lost the election will try to make the new party look bad.

I think about the many things that have happened in the past where we had to become united. We had to become the great nation that we are. We had to do these things because of emergencies. These emergencies, like the big wars, changed a lot of people's attitudes. Other wars, like Vietnam, changed a lot of attitudes, but this wasn't part of the united people that we say we are. To me, the war that I was involved in was a part of America.

I think a lot about this country that we have. It belongs to everybody. There shouldn't be no squabbling about it. Has our country learned by some of our bad mistakes? Many wars are going on yet. Why? I don't know. So much destruction of lives. For what reason? We had wars. We had indifferences. We had loss of many lives.

And what have we learned?

Inside the Walls

My grandmother had already passed on in 1947. All the time I was chasing around, she was sick and in the hospital. I had my truck and I went to see her.

She told me, "I don't want to die here, Grandson. I want to go home."

"They won't let me take you home." I even went and asked.

I told them, "My grandmother wants to go home."

"We can't let her go. She's on oxygen." She had pneumonia.

I went back and told Grandma, "They won't let you go. I asked them."

She wouldn't let me go. I stayed there quite a while — fourteen hours straight. I went to change my clothes and stuff, and while I was gone, she died. It was a sad time for me. It was hard for me to stay in Ferdinand and I guess that's why I just fell apart some more. It was like losing a part of your life right there. That's where I lost my direction.

My daughter Nellie was also born in 1947, but things never really did work out between her mother and I. It wasn't a good marriage. We were two different people with different backgrounds and different outlooks on life. I wanted to become a rancher. I wanted to raise cattle and farm, but she wasn't the type of person to get up early and stay up late. So we separated and later divorced.

That summer, in 1949, I got involved with a bunch of boys. We did a lot of bad things. We got caught for stealing tools, tires, and gasoline. It was all alcohol connected. You get too brave, run out of money, and you go ahead and do all these other things.

I met another women in my travels and she was half Nez Perce and half Blackfeet from Browning, Montana.

We lived together like man and wife, but we didn't get married. I tried very hard to farm. I bought a truck and she and I went over and worked in the peas. I tried and tried. Just never could make it work. After running with these other boys, we got into trouble and got hauled into district court. I was about twenty-four or twenty-five. They got us for larceny and sent three of us to prison. The judge sentenced us. I got a fourteen-year sentence.

It happened at Nez Perce, in Lewis County. Then they hauled us down to Lewiston for district court. We were in jail here. Then we got sent to the penitentiary in Boise. After we got down there, we were in quarantine a while. They put us out in the main part of the prison, what they call the main yard. Right there we knew we were in "the big time."

The first day we got out on the yard, we met—right away—some people that were Nez Perce that were there already. This old guy, his name was Pete. He came up right away and started talking to us in Nez Perce. He knew I could speak well and he talked to me right away.

Pretty soon he says in Nez Perce, "I got to go. I got some duties to do, but I'll be back."

Before he started to walk away he says, "Don't go anywhere. We're going to eat pretty soon."

It's an old Nez Perce saying. That really struck me funny. Like where could I go? That was a bad life. I just felt that there was nobody to blame but myself. I put myself there.

"How am I going to deal with this?" I thought

You see all kinds of people there. I started getting acquainted with some people there for life and some people there for short term. I met another man there.

During the time I was in the service I got a letter from

my mother telling me about this old guy that lived up on the prairie near Ferdinand. He was a white man. He lived alone, out in the country, and had gone into town. He didn't come to town very often. He didn't know there was a war on. He went to Ferdinand to buy groceries and supplies and the old guy at the store told him he had to have ration stamps. You had to have stamps for sugar and all kinds of things. This old guy didn't understand. The man at the store tried to explain it to him, but it made this old guy awful angry. He left and went home.

The next day, the guy went down to open up his store and the old man was in there. He had broken into the store and he had a gun. He was eating some things. The store owner didn't say anything, he just went ahead and started building his fire in the stove at the store. While he was building his fire, the old guy reared up and shot him. It was because there was a war on and he couldn't get it through his head that there was a ration requirement.

So there was a murder right there in Ferdinand during the war. I used to see this man a long time ago, but I didn't really know him. When I got in the main yard I asked around. I asked people if they knew Old Bill.

"Oh yeah. There's Old Bill, there."

I went up and introduced myself and I told him I was from Ferdinand, that I just got in. He was a big, strong, husky guy—kinda like a mountain man. He looked at me.

"Oh," he said. "You're Indian."

I said, "Yeah."

Right away he asked me about my uncle that lived in Ferdinand.

"Do you know Bart?"

"Sure. He's my uncle."

"Obed?"

"Yeah."

And he remembered Alvin. I told him Alvin died over in the Philippines. And you know that man got tears in his eyes? He had that much love for Indian people. I didn't know that. After that, everyday, I'd sit and visit and talk with him. He was a lifer. No hope for him to ever get out. He understood and he never would talk about it.

He'd ask me questions about other people that we both knew, but he never would talk about the town of Ferdinand. That was put aside from his memory. Once in a while I'd ask him if he had any money.

He'd say, "No."

I'd say, "Do you want ice cream?"

"Yeah." So I'd buy him ice cream.

I just tried to make the best of my time. We had to take IQ tests. They tried to classify you according to your IQ. This one man ran the main school in the prison. He was like the superintendent of all the different classes that people were in. I had to go before him and he reviewed my IQ test.

He said, "You got a pretty high grade here. Did you go to college?"

"No."

"Well, according to your IQ, you qualify with your knowledge."

I told him I had to take a lot of classes in the service as an engineer.

"Oh, now I understand. Since your IQ is so good, I'd like to have you teach school."

It was a shock to me.

"Well," he says. "You don't have to answer me right

now. Just think about it. Maybe in a couple of days you can come in and let me know."

When I got back out in the yard, I asked my friends about this offer.

"I got an offer to teach school."

"Hey, go ahead," they told me. "Go ahead. I think that's a good deal. You'll get to eat earlier and you'll get to do a lot of things. You'll get more privileges."

"Okay. I'll try it."

A couple days later I went up and I told this man, "Yeah, I'll go ahead."

"Good," he says. "I need a fifth-grade teacher."

He told me to report in the morning, right after main line chow—breakfast.

He said, "I'll have the students here for you."

The next day I had breakfast and then reported to the school. He took me into a little room and said, "Here's your students."

I walked in there and one of my own friends—the guy I got in trouble with—was sitting there. He was in the "fifth grade." We were together.

So I taught school. I had to teach them how to read and how to do arithmetic. It was a little different than teaching knot-tying classes in the service. Every once in a while, the superintendent would come in and listen to different things. I was given the assignments and I'd have to pass them along. My class was doing pretty good. I gave them all, maybe, ten minutes each on a book to read. They wanted everybody to read orally so I could correct them in the sound of the words. I was making headway and I got attached to it. I must've taught for a couple months.

When I had free time from school I used to go down to the music room. I never did learn to play anything, but I've always had this interest in music. This other man was named Gibb. He was an Indian man. He played quite a bit of music and he showed me things about the drums. He played the piano and I kept rhythm on the drums.

He said, "Boy, you got good rhythm."

I always did like music. We'd sit there and I'd drum for him. We passed a lot of time like that.

One day I got called out to the front office.

They said, "You're doing so well inside. We got an opening out here for Guards' Quarters." Janitor.

"The man that's been here was a lifer. He done a lot of time here, but he's going to be put on parole. We need somebody to take his place. We're offering this to you, because you seem to be doing very well inside."

I said, "Okay."

So I had the chance to go and be a trustee outside where all the food was better and you could sleep on regular beds. I had been in, maybe, six months, when I moved outside.

I fixed the guards' beds and even shined their shoes if they wanted them shined. A lot of them would leave change for me on their pillow, like maybe a nickel for a Coke. So I started having money. We could use what we called "hard money" out there in front, where inside the walls you had to use prison money. They were red-dish, brown-colored coins made out of some kind of fiber or something. They weren't made of metal.

I had pretty good relations with some of these guards. A lot of them had cars and I used to wash them for twenty-five cents a car. Also, the guy that had the position before me had waxed cars. People would come from the statehouse and bring their cars out to the prison to have them waxed. So I was getting them jobs, too. I was making $5.00 a car, besides the money I was getting from washing the cars.

All I had to do in the mornings was make up all the beds and gather up their laundry. I'd sweep their floors and send the towels inside to the main laundry. All this I had to take care of. I was going along pretty good there and I was making some money.

The rent money from my land was also accumulating and building up at the agency on the reservation. This is when my wife divorced me. While I was in prison she got custody of my two older children. They done all this when I couldn't defend myself in any way and I had to pay child support.

After eleven months in prison, I was eligible to go to the parole board. I went before them and they tried to talk me into staying for eighteen months and going for what they call a "straight kick." That's a full pardon. Or, if you thought you could go out into the world and follow all the regulations and all the parole rules—which were pretty much restricted—if you could live by those for six months, then they would give you a pardon.

I said, "Well, I'd like to try the parole." And they tried to talk me out of it.

"You'll never make it. You're too popular."

"I still would like to give it a chance."

"Do you have a place to go?"

I said, "Yeah, I have my aunt living in Ferdinand, where I was born and raised."

I gave myself a lot of time to think about things. Especially at night when they'd lock us up in these different dormitories. That's when I decided, "When I get out of this place I'm going to find me a job and get a home. Hopefully I can round up my kids, if they let me have them. Find somebody that I can depend on to be my wife. Hopefully, have more children. I don't want my kids to be alone like I grew up—by myself."

By this time, my third child, Purnell, was already a few months old. So many thoughts. I started making plans, started setting myself a pattern. "I wanted to do this . . . " Someday have me a car. I always wanted a new car. Everyday these thoughts became more intense. I kept wanting to see if I could do it.

The more I thought about it, the more I felt determined. My determination was building up. Finally, the time came for me to go out again. I had become friends with a lot of these people, these guards and deputy wardens—a lot of people. I have always had this knack of making friends, no matter where I was. The deputy warden took me to town one day.

He said, "We're going down and buy some clothes for you to leave with. The prison doesn't give you clothes like some places do. If you have money, you buy."

So we went shopping. He took me to a good clothing store and I bought me a pair of slacks, a good shirt, and a new pair of shoes. It was summertime and I didn't need a jacket.

When we came back I told them, "I'm all ready."

"Okay. Tomorrow morning you're out of here."

They brought me a guy I had to break-in and tell him what to do. I gave him directions and instructions: what guards to watch for because they were more lenient, and the ones that were having problems. I had one that worked in the office and he was becoming diabetic, but he didn't know it. A lot of times his bedding was wet. I changed the bed every day.

Finally he told me, "I'm going to go to the doctor."

I guess he got taken care of. His health became a little better and he stopped bed-wetting. I told the new trustee some of these guys need special attention.

"They're human beings," I told him.

Being in the prison is an experience I try to put way in the back of my mind. But still, at times, it does surface. I see a lot of my relations and young people making this kind of mistake, where you have to be confined to prison or jail. But we all understand it's a lesson. It's in your life record. You can't hide it. It's in your lifetime, in your past. I don't try to say that I've been a perfect man all my life. If I did, I would be telling a big falsehood. I don't think anybody's perfect. We all try to be perfect, but somewhere along the way we do bad things.

Alcohol can cause you to get in a lot of trouble. Especially for Indian people. Back in ancestral days, we never had this kind of element among our people. This was pretty much a clean continent or homeland. We didn't have this kind of thing that changes the personalities of people.

In the "old country," I guess alcohol was used for mostly social things, but when it got out here to the Wild West, it became a different thing. The settlers and the gold miners and all the other people that brought it here, they knew what it would do. I'm pretty sure they knew it would cause people to get drunk and what we call "give them false courage" to do different things. Of course it led to many things—murder. You might call it "the bad medicine." We just call it "strong drink" in Nez Perce. We've had so many things happen on our reservation because of alcohol.

We've had a lot of suicides. We've had a lot of murders. It's hard to talk about, because I have lost relations because of alcohol. Just for an example: I take care of the cemetery where my mother and grandmother are buried. And there, while I'm mowing the grass or cleaning up, I come by these other little markers. There I see that alcohol put him or her there. I consumed alcohol with these people, but didn't know that they were being overcome by it. They probably didn't realize, like I did, that this was our enemy. This was causing me to be in prison. So I had a chance to think about it and try the best I could to make a turnaround. I had a lot of time to give it complete thought—to run it through my mind. At the same time, I would see how many of our people had been overcome by alcohol, and how alcohol caused them to do really, really terrible things.

The bad medicine brought into our country is alcohol. It made a lot of our people do wrong things and it will still happen as long as it's being made. Every day you can read in the paper and magazines what it's doing. And on the next page you'll see it advertised.

On our reservation, alcohol is somewhat being brought under control. We're getting some highly educated counselors, some important people who study. A lot of them have gone through alcoholism and speak against it. Some people are overcome by alcoholism. I speak to some of them. I know they want to get out of it, but they just don't become brave enough to step up there and say, "I'm going to try." We let personal feelings overcome. They go back to the bottle and they think they can get the power to make themselves back to what they were. It's hard to make this turnaround. There's help now. Our tribal agencies are setting up these places for people to come and get help. All they have to do is go there and say, "I need help."

In the cell, at night or early in the morning, you wake up and think about your past. You think about "why this has happened to me." So you examine things in your mind and you come up with the answers—your own answers. You got to answer your own questions. I think a lot of us forget to do that. It is good to go out and ask people questions. Sometimes it's good to ask yourself a question and answer it yourself, your own way. So this is what I did.

After being behind the walls, you see people from all walks of life, all different nationalities in there for doing wrong—all different kinds of wrongdoing. Also, different attitudes. I learned so much about myself in there. They have psychiatrists, counselors, and chaplains in there, but you try to rehabilitate yourself in your own way while you're in there. Some people would just sit in the corner and sulk. They're against the world. They won't change.

There'll always be someone who is against the whole world. There will be people that will never change their ways. There will be people that will never rehabilitate. And they will tell you so. I've seen that with my own eyes. There's others that will try to tell you how you should be, how you should live. They mean that from their hearts, because they feel "If I were to have the chance, this is what I would do . . . ." But they're also the ones that will never get out of there.

I spoke to a lot of people. I made friends like I always do. The best thing I ever got from there was freedom. A lot of us will never know what freedom means until some of us get put away like that. I don't think any of us will. It's great to be in, what we called, "the Free World."

It wasn't easy. You come out of there and you're a marked person. Even right up to today I hear comments about my past.

"Oh, he thinks he's such a good person now, but I know when he was in prison." You hear that. A lot of times when I'm asked to do things or help out in some way, they say, "Why did they choose him? He's a marked person."

I still hear them thoughts, but it doesn't bother me anymore. I've made myself what I wanted to be—how I decided to be—when I was in prison. I made up my mind about what I wanted, what I wanted to do. I set a pattern in my own mind and heart. I come out of there with all of these positive thoughts and plans in my head.

'Course, it didn't work that way at first.

The deputy warden took me to the bus and told me, "I don't want to ever see you again." He said it in such a way that I knew he meant it, but I took it that he didn't want to see me again in prison.

I come to Lewiston where they had clothing stores and places where you could by things. It was a bigger town than Ferdinand with a bigger selection. I checked into a hotel. That evening I went to eat and then went to a movie. I hadn't been to a movie house for quite a while. And I ate popcorn. I sat there and watched the movie. I don't even remember what movie I went to.

When I got out of there, I walked down the street to my hotel and right there, right away, I got temptation. Some friends seen me walking and invited me into the car.

"Let's go for a ride."

They probably figured I had money and I did.

"I got a special appointment in the morning." I told

them I had to see the parole officer and I didn't want to be sent back to prison. I just used that for an excuse.

"Well, it's good to see you guys. You can let me off over here."

They let me off and they went on about their business. They were already drinking. I could've easily just said, "Let's go."

In your parole papers you're not supposed to even associate with people that use alcohol or drugs. I made a good move.

I went back to my room and I thought, "Well, I done something I don't think I've ever done: say no."

After that first time, when you refuse something, it's not that hard to refuse the next time. It felt good to me.

I came back to my home place. My uncle took me out to the old ranch where he had some cattle. We went out there and I spent the day walking around looking at the old places where I used to walk.

I told him, "Go ahead and go back into town if you've got something to do. I'll hike back in. I'm used to walking to town, anyway."

I spent my day out there, walking, hiking, resting, and thinking. I thought about the time I tried to farm when I first come out of the service. I thought about the time when I probably could've had this ranch going. Maybe these would be my cattle instead of my uncle's. A lot of these things run through my mind. But it all boiled down to: I got to find a job.

Getting Back

I finally got a job working for the old Nez Perce Railroad. It used to run from Craigmont to Nez Perce. I don't know why, but they were hiring Indian people. There were a lot of us that went to work there trying to rebuild that railroad, because the wheat farmers transported their wheat that way. That was before the trucking industry picked up. I worked there 'pert near all summer.

It got to the point where a lot of these Indian people began to wander off to different things like celebrations. Some of them would take off on the weekend and never come back. Then there were just three of us left. It was hard to get from Ferdinand to Nez Perce. I rode with this man and it seemed like we were late all the time. I was always ready, but he wouldn't pick me up till later.

We come to work there one morning and we were late. The foreman got mad and he told us he didn't want us anymore. So we left. I was disappointed. I was try-

to My Plan

ing to do some good. We decided to have a few drinks.
I was always paranoid about getting into trouble,
because I didn't want to go back to that place again.

This man was married to one of my cousins and he
kept saying, "I guess I should get home."

I told him, "Well, go ahead and go home. I'll be
alright. I can take care of myself."

It was fall time. First thing you know we ended up in
Orofino where they were having Lumberjack Days, I
started getting back into my old ways and not caring. I
felt myself slipping.

I ran into one of my cousins. He had come over from
Oregon with his uncle and some other people. He had a
nice car they were riding around in and they picked me
up.

I asked him, "What are you doing over here?"

He said, "I just come over with this uncle."

His uncle used to give him a lot of money, so he was

having a good time celebrating and having a party. Seems like when you want to find a party you can always find one. That's what happened to me.

Next thing you know, I was in Pendleton, Oregon. I was getting further and further back into my old ways — really slipping fast. Somehow the guy that worked with me at the railroad ended up down there and we were together again. We took my cousin back to Oregon with his uncle's car.

Coming back, we got to Dayton, Washington. We had a non-Indian with us. That was in the times when Indians couldn't buy liquor or beer. You had to have a "white man."

"I have a white man to go in and buy this thing for us to drink."

He was a vagabond. I guess he roamed the country a lot. My cousin and him got in a fight. I don't know what it was over. I think he sent him to the store to buy some wine and he didn't get the right change back or something. This man was drinking with us, too. They got into a hassle and the cops came. And there I was. I couldn't get out. I wanted to run away, but they grabbed me. I was still on parole when we got picked up.

I thought, "Well, I guess I'm in for it now. If they check up on me they're going to find out I'm on parole. They're going to hold me here until Idaho law enforcement people come and get me and take me back."

I didn't tell anybody I was on parole. This man that was married to my cousin had money. Not on him, but he had land in the Nez Perce area.

So he says, "If you let us bail out, we'll bail out."

They said, "You don't have any money."

"I can get money if you let me make a phone call."

They allowed him to make a phone call and he called this man who rented his land.

He said, "I want enough money to bail us out—all four of us."

The money got there real quick, in a telegram, and we got out before they even fingerprinted me or anything. I got saved by this man. When we got to Lapwai, there was a big gathering. They had tipis, stick game, and all kinds of things going on. I'm getting to look pretty terrible. I met one of my, what you call a "fall partner"—one of the guys that was with me when we got put in prison. I asked him for a change of clothes. We were about the same size and I got a pair of pants, a shirt, and a chance to clean up. Look a little decent, I thought.

I ran into one of my uncles from Ferdinand.

I said, "I want to go home."

We went home and in about two days I got myself back together. There was a new warehouse being built in Craigmont.

I said, "Let's go over there and get a job."

Three of us went over there and I talked to the foreman.

He said, "You guys come back. Report tomorrow morning. Seven o'clock, we start work here."

We worked there until the snow started flying. In the meantime, my uncle got a job with Potlatch Mill in Lewiston. It was in the veneer plant. They moved and got a place in Lewiston.

My aunt told me, "You might as well come and live with us and stay out of trouble."

I thought that was a pretty good idea. I moved in with them. The house they had was owned by a man who was a car dealer. He dealt with a lot with Indians. He'd sell cars from Lewiston, up to the reservation.

Everybody knew him as Jeremiah. He was a pretty nice man—a little crooked—but he was good. He could put you into a car, if you really wanted one, without a down payment, if he knew you had land or things like that.

This man wanted to make some repairs to the house. He brought the stuff and my cousin and I worked at it. On good days we'd work outside and bad days we'd work inside. That's the way we spent most of the winter. He'd take off some of the rent because we were doing this.

I tried to get back into the good way of life. I started going to church with my aunt. She was a Christian. We went to the Spalding Church. I got to going with them every Sunday. I was still young enough and I joined a Youth Group out there. We used to do a lot of things together, have a good time.

I also tried to visit my children from my first marriage. Their grandparents were raising them, because their mother had left them there. She had custody of them, but she wasn't taking care of them. One time I tried to see them and her parents wouldn't let me in the house. They opened the door and talked to me from the door.

"Oh, the kids aren't here."

I left. I guess they didn't want me to see them. I had money because I had worked and I wanted to buy some things for my kids. So I tried it again. Same thing. Finally, the grandmother told me that she didn't want her grandchildren to see me because I was a bad example.

She said, "You're probably drunk."

She just put me down. I didn't have much to say to that, because I thought I was bad. I wasn't claiming to be good, so I took that standing up. It made me feel bad, but I wanted to see my kids. What I really wanted to do was bring them to town and buy them some new clothes or toys. But I didn't get to do that.

And I said, "Well, I guess I deserved that. I had it coming."

I didn't know what else to do, so I come back and told my aunt what happened. The only way I could get something to my kids was I'd have to tell my aunt to take it to them. The grandmother wouldn't allow me to bring it myself. They were small, then. I don't think they remember this.

I also went out to the Potlatch Mill and applied for work. I kept going back all winter long, on Mondays, and asked if there was any openings. I wanted to work. On the 13th day of March, in 1951, I walked up to the place they call "The White House." One of my friends was with me and he filled out his application and we waited while it got processed.

A man said, "I'm going to put you guys to work today."

Boy, I felt myself getting back into my plan.

I thought, "This is a steady place of employment. I think I finally got my foot in the door."

He took us over to a place called the rough sheds, where they pile lumber, stack it, and store it. When they need it, they bring it out and process it. Sometimes these loads of lumber spilled and we'd have to re-pile them. We worked there for a week.

On Friday night, the foreman said, "I'll have to turn you guys over to the call board. You'll have to report to the personnel office again Monday morning."

On Monday morning we went out there. We sat there and they called my name.

"Axtell?"

I jumped up and he said, "You're going up to the sawmill."

At that time they had built this paper mill, and there

were a lot of personnel from the sawmill transferring over to the new paper mill. I think they were paying higher wages and a lot of the guys didn't like to work with lumber. So they were transferring and there were some openings in the sawmill. They took me up there by myself. They didn't call my friend's name.

They handed me a broom and a shovel. I was a cleanup man. It was the first time I'd ever been in a sawmill in my life. I didn't know what to do, what to watch out for. I seen all kinds of machinery. It was noisy in there. But I worked and I saw how lumber was being made. Sometimes I'd forget my work, and I'd stand there and watch the thing run. Watch it work and watch the lumber come through. How the logs were being sawed. I was really taken in by it.

I come home that night and I could still hear the buzzing of the mill. I was eager to go back to work the next day, because they didn't give me my card back. They gave you your card back when they didn't need you anymore. Friday night came and I didn't get my card.

I said, "Oh boy, I'm coming back here Monday."

It was like that for a couple weeks. Finally, one morning, here comes my friend. So we started working together. I didn't stay on the broom too long. I learned how to, what they called "picking edgings."

The longer I worked there, the more I wanted to know about it. One day they put me clear over on the other side of the mill as an "edgerman's helper." You had to be a little bit more coordinated. I was trying to learn and I was working harder and harder. I made some friends. I found out what kind of blood these lumber-jacks had.

Some of them come and talked to me like they knew me for years and were glad to see me. I was stepping into something that I think I'd been looking for. These guys were a different breed of people. To me, it felt like I was at home. It was just a good feeling to be there.

One day I come to work and this guy let his lumber pile up on him. He got rid of his boards, but he didn't make them according to standard, because he was poking them through there in a hurry, trying to get rid of them. The superintendent walked by and seen what was happening. They took this guy to the office.

He came back and said, "I'm all done. They fired me."

The foreman came over and he pointed at me. "Take that job."

I had never edged very much. I tried and tried. I'd come home so tired I couldn't hardly move. Finally, I started catching on a little bit. The other men came over and helped me. They showed me some of the tricks. Every little bit of information and instruction they gave me, I would keep in my head.

I realized I was fighting so hard to be able to do this that I was not trying to find an easy way. I was trying too hard. They showed me the easy ways and I started becoming an edgerman.

I didn't know the difference in the trees. I didn't know my species: the difference in the white and yellow pine, the white and red fir, and the tamarack. The only think I knew was cedar. I didn't know what dimensions I should make certain kinds of lumber.

This one Indian man, Alec, said, "Come back early at noon and I'll help you. I'll show you some things about edging."

I did that and it got to be a habit. I'd go back a little

early and then some other guy would come in there and help me. I was getting really attached to these guys, this mill, and all the people. It felt like I had come home.

I got a promotion. I started off as a common laborer at maybe, a dollar an hour, and then I was up to a dollar and a half. Then I found out about seniority. Somehow this one guy thought he was in line for this job. He made a complaint. I had to go by the regulations, the rules, so I stepped aside. But the man couldn't handle this job and they took him off and put me back on it. I learned all the different types of lumber that's got to be made from a certain species. I kept that job for twenty-some years.

After being there for quite a few years, the first thing you know I was teaching, and breaking in, other edger-men. I started showing my knowledge. Most of it is what I learned from the old-timers. They were teaching me about what they knew about the business. They were giving me the way to make myself better at being a lumberjack, being an edgerman. This has always been a part of my life—what I learned from the old people. This is what stays in your heart. It's always that way.

I became a member of the union. I became a helper in so many different ways. I helped with the community, where you give part of your wage to the "fund drive." I gave to the Boy's Club. I became engrossed by everything.

I got in with some Indian boys that worked at the mill and I told my aunt that I was going to move. I explained to her what we was doing.

We decided "We'll get us an apartment."

We pitched in together, four of us. We got this apartment. I started partying again, but we were still working. One day we got picked up and put in jail for disorderly conduct or something. My parole officer found out about it and they added six more months onto my parole. That was an extension, instead of taking me back to prison. What helped me was I was working and my work record was good, until that time. I was there every day. The parole officer made me move back with my aunt.

"Otherwise we'll either add more on to you, or we'll have to take you back. So you just think about it." He was a nice man. He was looking out for me in a good way.

At my aunt's house I met a woman from the town of Lapwai. She was full-blood Nez Perce and we got married. I was still trying to keep track of my children. I found out Purnell's mother had ended up marrying some other man and they were using a lot of alcohol and abusing my son, leaving him alone locked up in a trailer house for days. My aunt knew the people who told her these things. She went over to where Purnell's mother was living and asked her if I could have him. She agreed and let my aunt bring my son back.

My aunt brought my little boy home to me and my wife got very angry. She was a woman who couldn't have children and she got angry and left. My son was about four then, and I told her, "I want to keep my son." After about two weeks, she came back and said she would accept him and raise him. I think she had talked it over with her mother. She raised him very well. She took him to the doctor, sent him to school, and did everything that was necessary. She did everything for him. In fact, she spoiled him. She and I lived together like that for twelve years.

My cousin Leander and I were raised together when we were young. In later years, he got to drinking pretty

heavy and he got in trouble. He got put in the penitentiary at Walla Walla, Washington. When he was eligible
for parole, he needed someone to sponsor his parole and
a place where he could come and live till he got on his
feet with a job. He asked me if he could come to our
house and stay. I said yeah. He was like my brother, I
couldn't say no or turn my back on him.

He came and stayed in our spare bedroom. I was
working nightshift at the lumber mill. And I say a man
that's been locked up for a long time is going to make
advances at a woman. I guess that's what happened.
One morning I came home and got into bed. Next to
me, my wife said, "No, no, no. He's going to be home
from work pretty soon." I couldn't figure out what she
meant. Finally, it dawned on me what was going on. I
laid there and tried to sleep. The next day, I approached
the both of them about what was happening. They
probably figured I would never find out, but I did. I
told them if they wanted to do that then they couldn't do
that in my house. I told them both to leave. Later on we
divorced.

It was in the fall of 1963 and I got rather broke up
over our divorce. We had a good life, a clean life. We
never drank. I thought it was a decent living that we put
together. My being good to Leander—concerned about
his life after being out prison—broke all of us up. After
that I stayed home a lot. I wouldn't go hardly anyplace.
Purnell stayed with me, because he didn't want to leave
with her. She went on her way and I was alone again.

I wasn't sure if I wanted to get married again. I was
making a lot of different decisions in my mind. When I
was incarcerated, I had a plan and this plan included
having more children. I wanted to have a good wife, a

good family, a good home and a good car. I thought I had it there for a while, but that ended. I became pretty paranoid about marriage then. I realized that things can happen very quickly. It got to the point where I thought it was impossible to find the perfect woman.

One Sunday morning I got a phone call. It was a few months after I'd gotten divorced. A woman I knew called and told me her daughter had recently had some of the same problems I had. Her daughter had recently been separated and divorced from her husband in Arizona. This woman said she would like to have me meet her daughter, Andrea.

"But," she says, "you think about it."

I went to work that day and thought about what she said. I knew the concerned mother very well. When my mother died she was married to my stepfather, Fred. After she died, Fred ventured out and married Andrea's mother, the one who eventually called me. I also knew Andrea's father real well. He was a nice man who lived over in Nez Perce, Idaho. The reason I knew him was he used to be my mother's boyfriend before Fred came along. So that's how things got put together. It was a long connection.

I sat around the house and began to forget about what had recently happened to me — the broken marriage, the divorce and all that. Some of the bitter memories left me and I started thinking ahead.

I wondered, "Are these things going to work for me again?"

One day I was sitting at home watching the Army/Navy football game with my ex-wife's nephew. He had come over to watch the game with me. We talked and laughed together. Her brother was also good to me. They used to come visit with me all the time. After the game, they left. Then my kids Nellie, Chuckie, and Purnell came to the house later that afternoon.

They said, "Dad, why don't you go someplace? Just don't sit around. Go to a movie or something."

They wanted to go to a dance, so I took them. As I was driving across the bridge I was thinking. The next thing I knew I was going up toward Kamiah where Andrea and her mother lived. I thought it might be a good time to go and meet her. I went to their house like a gentleman. Andrea wasn't home. She was in town with her sister. Their mother took me to where Andrea was and brought her out to meet me.

She said, "Well, I'll leave you two alone."

We started talking and talked most of the night. I found out she had three little daughters. I told her I had three teenagers. Things were being talked about in a positive way. I left my old truck parked out in front of this place where we had met and went over to her house. I laid on the couch to sleep and she went on up to bed upstairs. In the morning I got the feeling somebody was watching me. I opened my eyes and saw three little girls peeking at me from around the piano. They all still had their pajamas on. When I opened my eyes they pulled back.

I said, "Hello. Good Morning."

The oldest one had already been in school. She talked to me. The two other little ones ran back upstairs. I sat up and talked to Kay, the oldest little girl. Pretty soon she ran over and got a book. It was getting close to Christmas, so I had to read the Christmas story to her. When I got done she said, "Read it again." I don't know how many times I read it.

Andrea and I got pretty involved together. We got

very close and started talking more and more about the future. She had been badly hurt from her first marriage. I guess some of the things that we learned in the past brought us together. I was driving up the river from Lewiston to Kamiah to see her. She met my children and I loved her children. One day I asked her if she thought about making a family together.

I said, "I guess what I'm saying is I'm proposing to you. You think about it."

I drove home and got ready for work. One afternoon, just before I was going on my shift, she called me and asked me if I still had things on my mind. I said yes.

She said, "Well, let's do it."

That afternoon we set a date. "This weekend," she said.

We applied for a marriage license. We went to a Presbyterian minister at Kamiah and asked if he would marry us. I had known this man all my life and he said, that, according to the church rules and with both of us recently divorced, he couldn't marry us. Oh, he gave us quite a few reasons why he couldn't perform the wedding. We decided to see a judge I knew. My kids been before her a few times when they'd gotten into trouble and I had them released to me. So I called her up and told her what had happened with the man we had asked to marry us.

She said, "Just come on up and bring a couple of witnesses. I'll do this at home right now."

It must have been about 8:00 or so at night. It was a Saturday night on December 21st. Andrea had just turned twenty-four on the 21st of October and I had turned thirty-nine on the 7th of November. I was fifteen years older than her. The kids went somewhere else that night and Andrea and I spent our evening together at home. Our next-door neighbor was a real good friend and he tried to be nice. He'd bring stuff over to us and we really didn't want any company, you know? Every little while he was knocking on the door.

"Do you need some coffee?" he said.

We're weren't even thinking about coffee.

Andrea and I had a good start, but our struggles began not too long afterwards. Finances were pretty hard. She was paying on her station wagon. I was paying on my pickup, because the car that my former wife had taken was completely paid for. We were paying on two rigs and making house payments. It got pretty hard. Andrea went to work for the BIA at Lapwai, on the reservation. We had to hire a babysitter to sit with our youngest kids. Things got tough, but I had found a woman who would stick it out no matter how bad things got. Andrea was young, and well, things didn't go straight for awhile. She had her problems. She mixed in with people that would party and things. This almost tore us apart. It caused me to go back to the use of alcohol again—after, maybe, thirteen years. We even talked about separation one time. Her mother—the one who brought us together—sensed something was wrong and she came and lived with us for awhile. She got us back on track.

It's My Turn

In Lewiston, Idaho, before I went into the service, they used to have signs in a few restaurants saying, "No Indians Allowed." That was some of the segregation I remember. The biggest problem was with the law. We're always the first to be arrested. I hate to say it, but that's the way it is. I've lived here for quite a while and I've seen a lot of things happen with segregation and discrimination.

I've had this experience many times where I had to say a few things back when I was put down by certain people about my being American Indian. I didn't raise my voice or use bad language. All the times that I've been to any place, I'm always proud to say that I'm American Indian.

This reminds me of the time I went to El Paso, Texas, to gunnery school when I was in the service. We were taking classes on .50 caliber machine guns and we got a chance to go into town on pass. So we went over into

Juarez, Mexico. We crossed a bridge and walked over. When we were checking in, everybody had to say their nationality. So all my friends were going in and the border agents come to me and asked me what I was. I said, "American Indian." I kind of hollered it out. I guess I felt so good about being an Indian.

My friends thought that was pretty good. "You must be proud of what you are." I was the only Indian in our company. I always said to myself, "I'm a Nez Perce." I never, ever thought about turning my back on my tribe and I never will.

People don't overlook me like they used to. I seen this happen—even to me—maybe fifteen years back. It happened several different places down here in town. I'd be standing there waiting my turn and they'd overlook me and ask this other guy, "What do you want?" And I'd be standing there thinking, "I was already in line."

My two grandchildren and I went in to get ice cream. People were coming in, getting their orders. We were still standing there. Finally, my granddaughter said, "Grandpa, how come we gotta wait so long?" You know how little kids are. All the people looked around and they seen us standing there for quite a while. It kind of embarrassed the people so they come and waited on us. Things aren't quite like that anymore. Now when it's my turn, it's my turn.

Andrea and I helped out in a lot of different things when our kids were in school. We also changed some things. One of the things was that a school here had textbooks describing American Indian people that were not agreeable to us. By phasing them out we made it a little easier for our children to go to school so they wouldn't be looked at in the way some of these books were describing Indian people. It wasn't nothing really, really serious, but it still wasn't proper. We got involved.

Also, when the Sacajawea Junior High School in Lewiston, Idaho, chose their mascot, they came up with the name "Savages." That didn't seem right for us to be called savages. I don't think the word should be used for anything like that anymore. We went to bat and showed our concern. We done it in a good manner, through the proper channels with common courtesy. It came through and we changed it. Now they're the Sacajawea Braves, which shows a lot more dignity to the Indian people. My children went through that school and it's a good school. I have no negative feelings about the school.

As far as I know, we've never had an American Indian on the school board here in Lewiston. Maybe there's a reason for that and maybe there isn't. I don't know. Will they have to go through all the tension that we did?

How long is this going to last? It may be a good thing if we did have an American Indian school board member because there are quite a few American Indian students that are going to school here and many of them have graduated and gone on to college.

It's hard to sit down and give instructions to younger people. So many modern things are happening. Of course, we like to see our young people get educated. We strongly believe education is very important. Back in the old times when I grew up, there were a lot of people that never finished school. I was fortunate that I was close to school. My mother also went to school. Out there in the old country school, Leander and me were the only Indians. After a time, when things started getting better, several of my Indian friends stayed with us and went to school with me for awhile.

Coming Back

When I changed over to my present religion, the Seven Drum Religion, I really got a lot of strength from the Long House in Nespelem, Washington. A certain man helped me. He was my elder. A lot of times I needed a little instruction or I got in a predicament. Modern times gave us a quicker way to communicate. We didn't use the old smoke signal that much anymore. We got on the telephone and I got the advice I needed. He told me, so I did it. It felt comfortable. I didn't feel puzzled or anything, because I did it the way I was instructed.

At times I've been told that some of the things that I was instructed by an elder to do were wrong. It makes me feel as though my elders were being criticized. Not only like this man I mentioned, but further back — maybe his elders and the elders before his elders. The connection goes way, way back.

Andrea and I had a beautiful aunt — an elder — named Helen. We all called her Aunt Helen, even our kids.

t o   t h e

I n d i a n   W a y s

She became our advisor while we were still involved in the Presbyterian religion with Andrea's mother and my father. She told us what we needed and had to do when our daughter was asked if she would run for royalty in the *'Ipetes* Powwow. It usually occurs in the spring time. We came home and talked about it and our daughter decided she wanted to try it.

Our aunt said, "She has to have all these good things to make her look good."

In the Indian way she had to have a buckskin dress and many other things. We didn't have any of that. Maybe a few beaded bags. We had to teach her how to dance. She caught on real easy. It's not hard to teach an Indian person to dance.

Aunt Helen said, "We're gonna grab this whole thing by the horns and go at it."

So we went after it. We done everything that was necessary by giving her an Indian name and getting all the regalia. We followed the instructions of our elder. Besides that, she was starting to talk to us about a lot of other things. She was making us understand that the Indian way of life is so very important. The Indian way of life was out there. Of course, I knew a lot of this already, growing up with my uncles and learning a lot of things about the old ways from my grandaunt who was a medicine woman and a lot of other people who encouraged me.

The final day of the powwow came and our daughter won. She became queen of the '*Ipetes* Powwow. When a person wins a position like that they have to go to different powwows and represent this powwow. This drew us closer and closer to the powwow trail. Then, our younger ones were beginning to see a lot of this dancing and they're beginning to like it—the whole family, myself, even Andrea. But we were still connected with the church. We respected my mother-in-law's and my father's Christian religion and the way we grew up. I still helped my dad because he was elder of the church up at Ferdinand. But we did kind of cover up our involvement with the powwows. We didn't feel like we were doing anything wrong, but we didn't want our parents to feel bad about it. The Christian religions didn't think too much of powwows. We'd tell Dad we were going somewhere for the weekend and we'd load up our Indian regalia. It was kind of hard at times to bring stuff out to the car. I think Dad knew what was happening, but he never did say anything.

He became very ill. One time he had a nosebleed that wouldn't stop and he got pretty weak and I called the ambulance. They took him to the hospital. He got very angry at me, but they saved his life. Another time, Andrea made an appointment for him to see the doctor.

She didn't tell him, though. Dad liked to go shopping for groceries or anything, just to go to the store.

She said, "Well, do you want to go to the store?"

He said, "Yeah" and jumped in the car.

Instead of going to the store she pulled up in front of the doctor's office and said, "Dad, I made an appointment for you."

He said, "No, no, no."

She said, "This is for you because we love you. We want you to get doctor care and get the to the source of your illness. Maybe they can help you become a little more able instead of feeling sick all the time."

They sat there and she talked to him for quite a while. Finally, she talked him into going in to see the doctor. Dad had bronchial asthma and diabetes. After he began treatment, he became active again. Andrea prolonged his life, maybe, twenty years, by taking him to the doctor.

The younger ones wanted to dance. We couldn't deny them because what we do for one we have to follow through for the rest. We started getting outfits for them to dance in. What's the use of dragging them around the powwow if they can't participate? So that drew us a little closer and closer to the Indian way of life and it was beginning to fit in so beautiful. It was just happiness.

Aunt Helen kept talking to me and Andrea about different things. Beyond just dancing. She's beginning to show and teach Andrea a lot of things about the Indian way of life. How to be a person that cooks and plans for feasts and big dinners. How to go to different places and dig roots and how to go and pick huckleberries and cut salmon and do so many things. She could do all this. Andrea had this beautiful teacher to teach her these things and she uses that talent today. I'm glad she learned so well. She taught Andrea everything that is connected with Indian feasts and Indian preparation of foods. She never left anything out. Aunt Helen gave her instructions on how to be a strong woman, how to treat your husband, and help your husband.

She was talking to me at the same time. She told me, "We need a leader. Our Indian religion is gone. Nobody does it anymore. I been talking with some other ladies and men. You are a good man. You work hard. You have a good family. You get involved in the Indian way of life. You speak your language real good. We want you to learn the Indian way of worship. We want you to be our leader."

She always insisted, "That is the kind of leaders we need in our tribe—the ones that know the language and can speak the way our old people spoke, and bring out the words that the old ancestors spoke to relate these ways that we have. To relate the ways of our people, to relate to the dancing.

"But," she says. "You think about it."

She kept telling me these things. When you're approached by someone you strongly respect—the way we respected her—you become very serious. You think about the things she tells you. This began to work on my mind.

I also started to learn the songs. That was automatic. It was starting to fit into my way of being part of the dancing circle because my children were dancing. I started drifting away from Christianity.

The time came to have the Root Feast in the spring-time. There was nobody on our reservation to run the Long House, but the ladies still used to go and dig the roots. Then they'd get together and invite people from Nespelem or Yakima, Washington, to come sing and do things for the Root Feast. This man came from

Nespelem to do the singing and leading of the services and he brought his singers. There were some people that came from the Yakima Valley, too. I guess they all felt the need for this religion to become alive again on this reservation.

At this feast, I helped my aunt. Both Andrea and I did. Whatever she wanted me to do, I did. She was working me in there pretty good. She always made me serve the coffee and things like that. I wasn't just jumping right into it. I was taking my time. I started doing more of these things. Doing these special things — these special ceremonies — began to enrich our values. It enriched our thoughts about our children and we felt how connected we were becoming. So many things entered our lives that way with the direction of our Aunt Helen.

One day she says, "I want you to grow your hair. All leaders must have long hair."

Again she told me, "We need a leader. We have nobody to do our religion." There were many other concerned people who felt like my Aunt Helen.

I told Andrea what Aunt Helen said — what she wanted me to do and to be. I wasn't going to do anything until we talked about it. It's that way now. I don't make decisions by myself and she doesn't either. We talked and debated it for a week, I guess.

Andrea said, "If you're willing, I'll go along with you."

I decided I would go ahead and start letting my hair become longer. I felt the difference in the Indian way of life. It felt good, stronger. I guess you could say it was like finding yourself. This really wasn't in my plan when I was in prison, but it looked good to me. It felt good. She told me to let me hair grow and the longer it grows the more respect and power you get. Sometimes, in the traditional ways, you never cut your hair. My wife braids my hair. If she passed on, then I would cut them off. It's like a show of respect to your wife who handled the hair.

Ever since I've grown my hair long and wear it in braids, people will get surprised that I can speak English. We went one place last year, my wife and I, and this man came up and wanted to ask me a question.

He asked my wife, "Can he speak English?" And this man was an Indian man.

To me, it was a compliment. It really makes me feel good when I hear things like that. They're not doing it to make me feel that I'm ignorant. It's the respect they have for this hair that I have. It makes me feel dignified to be classed like that, to be looked upon as a real Indian and that's a good feeling.

When Andrea and I got involved in the Indian ways, it made us become so strong. We became more attached. We became more understanding with each other. But in the beginning, we really didn't trust one another. We overcame that. Some of the most important advice was given by her mother.

She said, "You can't let the hardships overcome you."

Aunt Helen also told us not to be jealous if someone shows interest in your wife or in your husband.

She said, "You should be proud someone is taking a liking to your wife or husband. It shows that you are standing out."

You see a lot of these talk shows where people are talking about jealousy. They talk about cheating on one another. Some people say how good it is to have an affair on the side. If you're going to love someone for the rest of your life, you got to build your resistance against all these kinds of thoughts or else they will overcome you.

You have to talk things over. Sometimes I get a little discouraged and wonder why she didn't want me to do something, and later on, it will hit me why. Usually she is right. Sometimes she'll come to me with a certain problem and we work it out together. Once in a while, some of our children are not doing the right thing and it bothers her. One of the things that hurts me the most is to see her cry. You can tell how much she loves her grandchildren and her children when she comes to me and begins to weep deep down in her heart. We console one another. I have the same problem when my heart is broken by some of my elders going away to The Good Land. I get lonely by memories of the war, memories of my childhood. We lean on one another.

In order to make things happen in a good way, you've got to think and work together. I know it's sometimes hard to give in and say, "I was wrong," but that's one thing you've got to learn to do: admit you've made a mistake. I've had to do that. I've admitted I was wrong and she has admitted to me. We don't make a big deal about that anymore. You can't expect two people, even if they've been married for so long, to have the same thoughts. We got to open up our minds. When I have a suggestion and she has a suggestion, we talk about it. I give her my plan and she gives me her plan. First thing you know, we got one good, strong plan worked out. I don't say, "My plan is better than yours." We don't talk that way. If our plan is wrong, then we're both wrong. If it's right, then we're both right. A lot of people don't realize that deciding together, whether it be something minor or major, helps things fall into place. The old Indian people taught us to live every day like it's our last day. We never know when things are going to happen.

We do a lot of things together. We like to go away

from the everyday work for a little bit and just be alone. It makes a lot of difference. We don't sit at home and sulk. When we decide to go somewhere, we go. We leave everything—all the worries and stuff—behind. I get her away from reality for a little bit. I get her away from cooking, washing dishes, and keeping house. She deserves it. We don't dominate one another and we don't abuse one another in any way. It's a good life. I know it won't last forever, but we'll make it last as long as we can.

I'm a very fortunate man to have a woman like Andrea. It's hard to find someone like her. I tell people how much I love my wife and I tell my Creator that every day. I thank Him for bringing us together. I tell her how much she means to me. If the time comes and we have to part, it's going to be difficult. But we know we can't live forever. In my heart, she's the most beautiful person I have ever met. I want people to know this: She's the one who made my life what it is now.

We have a lot of beautiful things to look back on. We have a good time thinking about a lot of things that we've done, all the places we've been. It takes a lot of wisdom to make things happen, especially wisdom from the ones who told us how we must live, wisdom to realize what our Creator has done for us. How we must discipline our children. Ourselves, mainly.

I have a lot of honor for the people that were very, very helpful in my struggles in becoming a leader in the Long House. They supported me. I always remember them whenever I go to the Long House to sing. It's people like these that I think of when I do my spiritual things in the Long House. This is very important: To remember special people like that. There are many others that have given me good words, strong words. I always remember the words of a lot of older people—the ones that taught me to sing songs and corrected me. Sometimes, I make a little mistake in singing the song, and they'll come and give me the proper ways to do these things. Not that they're criticizing me in any way, that's just the way our Indian people are.

Same way with the language. You make a mistake, they don't tell you. They just casually come and say the word the right way and you take it from there. It seems like you remember things a lot more that way. It sticks in your mind. Whereas, if it was done in a different manner, you'd kinda turn your back. You'd turn if off a little bit in your mind, but when things are done in such a beautiful way, you never forget it.

Annie, the elder we called Grandma, gave me a lot of instructions. I think she was the last one on the reservation that was what we call "of the old way." She couldn't read, write, or speak English, but she had strong medicine powers. She wore her moccasins and wing dress everyday. Always. When she went to town, or anyplace, she would wear a shawl and muffler just like the old people that I remembered.

Every time I went to the Long House to open it up and build the fire, she would come over. Sometimes it'd still be cold in the Long House, but she wanted to come over and talk. She wanted to sit there with me and talk the Nez Perce language. I always made her laugh and that's why she would come over. She liked for me to explain things to her, things she'd heard. She had very, very strong beliefs and strong powers, because Elsie, her stepdaughter, told me she could foresee a lot of things. They always come out the way she would tell them.

"So many people are going to be here today." She'd tell us how many.

"The weather is going to be a different thing." She'd tell us what kind of weather.

She never did call me Horace. She called me "*miy-ooxat*," which means leader or boss. She'd always be telling people, "He's going to be good. He's going to be good, because I want him to be good. I want him to be strong."

She was very, very strong in this religion. Her brother was a Presbyterian minister, but she hung on to her old ways. She stayed that way all her life. She always told me that she was very, very happy that some-one had taken up this religion again.

She said, "I used to think about it when nobody would lead or make us get together." She was very happy that someone had taken it upon themselves to try to bring this religion back into the reservation. She never did say why she thought the religion was being lost. I think a lot of it was because of the Christianity that came in. She never did blame Christianity, but she always referred to them as "the other people." Then she would speak about our religion being so important. She was always speaking to us about the new day, the light, and the things of nature—the snow, the rain, the thunder. She could say so many beautiful things, just about anything Nature does. It was a thrill to have her talk. A lot of times I use some of her philosophy when I'm speaking to young people. It just comes out the way Grandma used to say it.

Don't Call

Although I'm a leader in the Long House and I hold respect for the position, a lot of places call this leader the "chief." I feel, myself, that I don't qualify to have that title. The place where I was called a chief was in the army. Seems like all the Indian people were "Chief." I told them, "Well, I wish I could've been a chief. It's a very high position. He's a soldier that has leadership qualities."

I think that one of the best things that ever happened on our reservation is that we got our hunting and fishing rights back. One of the other things given was the right to buy liquor and go into bars. It created a problem and it's still a big problem yet. But I still think that the warriors who served under General Eisenhower deserved these rights. Nobody could see why they couldn't have the privilege of going into a bar or buying liquor. They laid their lives on the line to protect their country.

One day, after all these laws passed, I took my dad

Me Chief

out for a ride way up in the mountains. I like to remember this because it was the last deer that he ever shot. We come around this turn up by Weitas Meadow and saw a buck standing there, looking right at us.

"Dad, there's your buck."

He grabbed my old .30-.30, jumped out of the pickup, and shot. He knocked it down. Boy, he run over there, grabbed that deer and dragged it into the woods. We heard a car coming. Dad was in the woods and laid down beside the deer.

"What are you doing, Dad?" I said.

He laughed, "Oh, I forgot. We can hunt and fish legally."

He was going back to the old days when our old people used to have to do that—poaching, I guess. He got quite a charge out of that because he was so used to having to hide.

"Don't have to do that now," I said. "It's all legal now."

We used to laugh about that. That's just an illustration about what we had to go through. Some of my people still talk of going hunting and having to buy licenses. There's always a lot of things said about our rights. I think a lot of it is that non-Indian people go out there and slaughter for trophies, not food. We didn't have enough to eat. That's what our old people had to do back in the old days. Sometimes hunting days at a time, not getting anything. The weapons and things they used in the old days weren't modern like they are now. You hear a lot of negative things, like some of our younger people have four-wheel drive rigs, high-powered rifles, and the advantage that we have. I tell my people to use these things. Once in a while there are some of our people that get careless and sell some of their meat. Not everybody does that.

I had a non-Indian neighbor that was having a hard time. He had a family and he was out of work. After it became legal for us to hunt and fish, I went hunting and got a couple deer. I usually tried to get two or three so I could give to the old people that couldn't go out and hunt. When I brought my deer back, I kept thinking about my neighbor that was having a hard time. So I went over and asked him if he would accept this deer from me. I took it to his house without anybody seeing me.

"If anybody says anything, you tell them I gave it to you."

We talked about it for awhile and he said, "You know Horace, I'm having a tough time."

"Yeah, I know that."

One day, when this man got back on his feet, he brought me something that he valued. It was hard for me to accept it.

He said to me, "I can see by the way you handle your-self and your family and the discipline you show, what kind of person you are. I got something here that I know you can use. I've had this for quite awhile."

He give me a clock, one that you wind. He give it to me from the heart. He became a real neighbor. It wasn't too long after that he and his family left the country. I had that clock here until my little ones knocked it over and broke it.

One of the teachings of our old people was that we shared. We shared and we gave. It never was easy, but we always gave thanks for everything we had. We still do that. Especially when young men do traditional things, old things. I feel good when my nephews come and bring me a hindquarter of deer or elk. Other people bring me a jar of huckleberries.

Washington, D.C.

Andrea and I were in the second largest hotel in Washington, DC. We got on the elevator. I had my eagle staff in a tube. Some people got on the elevator. A guy asked, "Going fishing?"

I said, "Yeah. I'm going fishing and I want to catch some suckers. I hear they got a lot of big ones over here."

He kind of resented that. Finally he said, "Well, I guess you're right." When he said that, all the people in the elevator all broke out and laughed. So I guess he took it okay.

The tribal office on our reservation was asking people why they wanted to be in the Inaugural Parade, why did they want to go. One of the things I said was I was a member of the Nez Perce Tribe. A full-blooded Nez Perce on my mother's side and my father's side, full-blooded all the way. I wanted to represent my tribe because I'd represent the old people. Not the present, but the past. The directions of what the elders had taught us. Also, I wanted to represent my tribe because I'm a veteran warrior. I wanted to represent not only the warriors of today, but the ones that fought for some of our traditions, our culture. The concerns I have in my heart are for what we have, what we received from our past. What is our future going to be? Just sit back and not participate? That's one of my concerns. I wanted to represent all the warriors, because I'm a veteran of WWII and I spent some time in the South Pacific. I know the hardships warriors go through.

"Besides," I said. "I'm a Democrat." It's an honor to parade in front of the president.

A particular person — someone who has feelings for the Indian way of life, the understanding of the Creator and Mother Earth — paid for my wife and I to go to the Inaugural Parade. I didn't think something like this would ever happen to me. She was there when we sang our religion songs by the Wallowa Lake in Oregon. She could almost picture how the old people used to live in the Wallowa Valley. She is not an older person. She is very nice to talk with and will always be included in my prayers. People are making us feel important by acts like this.

About 11:30 or so, President Clinton got sworn in. Soon as he got sworn in, the cannons fired. There were a lot of fireworks. Luckily, one of the trainers was hanging on to the rope of my horse. Sam's horse took off across the square at a full gallop. He managed to stay on. He got it stopped and came back. He said, "I wasn't about to let go. I just wasn't about to get bucked off." He did good. I was proud of him.

So many people were watching the parade. Like when you go to a football game and you look up in the stands and you see all these people. You can't hardly pick anybody out. The bleachers were full and the people were waving American flags. I got to one group of young kids and they were waving their flags. I waved my feather fan and they let out a big cheer. That was nice. There were a lot of other people that clapped for the Nez Perce people as we went by and waved. I heard my name hollered, "Hey, Horace!"

Along the way, there were these tall scaffolds way up high. Cameras were set up. We were going by there and my horse had a trainer in case something happened. He was just walking alongside. He said, "Over there, Horace. You're on national TV." I looked over and I started waving. That's where I was, on MTV. My grandson saw me on MTV because he watches it a lot.

When we went by the President, I was on one side and he was on the other. The trainer said, "Oh, look over to your left." I looked over and I seen the President.

I started waving my feather fan. Just as I did that, he looked down at his paper. He didn't get to see me. It was still a good feeling to ride in front of the president. I was honored to be a part of it. I probably had more feelings than a lot of people that participated. Some of them were there just to be there. This was a chance of a lifetime for me. I wore my best buckskin, my best war bonnet, and I had an Appaloosa to ride.

When the party of our government changes, seems like all Indian people are looking for change. Some of the things that happened in the past were not right. We come out on the bottom end of a lot of things. So we look for new things to happen to our American Indian people. I hope this will be the time we will be given some attention. Will it be wait and see or wait and see some more?

When You

Speak from

All the things that they taught me, there's nothing written down. I experienced this. When you talk to a person you tell them. Instruct them. You want them to know you talk with your heart. When you talk from your heart it goes up out of your eyes, into the other's eyes, and comes back down into their heart. That's the way these stories and instructions were told to me. Look at somebody in the eyes when you talk to them, when you really want them to understand. Give them advice. Maybe they done something a little bit wrong and you want to correct it. The proper way to correct somebody is to look right into their eyes and then it goes into their heart and stays there.

It goes from one heart to another heart and it keeps going around like that. That's the way our old people did it and that's the way I think about all the things that I do now. The old ones passed it from heart to heart — back and forth. That's the way I was told. When you

t h e   H e a r t

give knowledge in the Indian ways, it shows that you believe that it means what they said. Everything was done with a good feeling, but if you done bad things, discipline was done the same way.

They'd say, "Look at me. I want to talk to you."

So you sit there and you don't say anything back. You just keep quiet. When they get to a certain point and they want to make you understand, their voice changes and becomes like, ready to cry, it gets so intense. That's when you know they are very sincere. Their voice gets shaky.

"Listen."

You listen. Then you can feel the tears come out of your eyes and you know the feelings that they've given you. They stay there. It's so intense. You remember, if you take the wrong steps again, about that guy or that woman. You don't do it. That's why I feel the way I do about a lot of things—the way I interpret people and the way I was taught. To love one another, always be concerned, try not to turn your back on people, always help. Always help.

We were taught to watch our grandparents do things so we followed what they did to survive. It was hardly any problem to survive—to be able to pick enough roots and berries to make your way. Now it's tougher. Different foods are scarce. Roots are scarce. All the other things are hard to find now.

The life that we have is the life that we want to hold on to—our Indian ways. These ways were left here from our old people. Our ancestors done it that way—one heart to the other. It's still here. You can trace this back. The non-Indian population is beginning to see what life was like back in the old, old times. These people want to learn and understand who the Indian people were. They ask me questions. A lot of them are questions about the old history that I can't answer. I don't claim to be a historian. I don't claim to be a consultant of any kind. I can only tell them what I learned from my elders and old people. The strong beliefs are still being carried on about the rules being used the right way. We're trying to uphold these old instructions by our elders that were passed on down through the generations—how we uphold the spirituality, how to keep it strong.

It's just what I learned in my childhood, living a life that was taught to me.

> How to live a life.
> How to present yourself.
> How to behave.

All these things fall into place. This is what gives me the honors that I get from people nowadays. You don't have to advertise. You don't have to go and make a name for yourself by advertising your abilities or advertising that you are a well-to-do person or a well-mannered person. It comes by itself. People will see this without reading about your past. You display these things with who you are and what you are. Many times you help people with, maybe, just one or two words.

I'm still learning. I always tell my younger people, "I'll keep learning until I close my eyes for the last time." That's the way I look at life.

Do what your heart wants you to do. Understand these procedures about how our old, old people had believed—how they worshipped on the seventh day, kept their bodies clean, minds clean, and hearts open to instruction. Also, to pass on the knowledge and wisdom to the young people.

Whenever I have a chance, I ask the Creator for a little bit of the wisdom that our old people had. I ask the Creator for some of the wisdom my great-grandfather and my great-grandmother had, along with what I've learned from my elders already. I think that all this put together helps you do a lot of things.

As far back as I can remember, this has always been a teaching: The elders are always the ones that have the wisdom. They have the teachings about things from elders further back. The older people are always thought to be the role models of our tribe. Many of us talk about them a lot.

Sometimes we have different gatherings like a Name Giving, a memorial, or a funeral. The elders will come out and talk. They always talk about their elders and what their elders learned from their elders. This is carried on. I used to hear my grandmother talk about her elders all the time. I guess it's always been that way.

When a person's hair begins to get pretty gray and light, they are becoming elders. We tried to be like the elders that we looked up to. So this is the message that is being put across to the young people today: We respected our elders. When you respect someone, show your respect. You'll get respect back. That's the way I see it.

Respect yourself. If you don't have any respect for yourself, you won't have any respect for anybody or anything else. The Creator made us to be a part of this world. You got to look at yourself first, then you can see the Creator made you and everybody else for a certain reason.

Have respect for rain, the snow—the weather. The weather is something the Creator gives us. It's a gift. He gives us water to revitalize us. It gives us a refreshing feeling. Sometimes we get a little disturbed when we get caught in the rain. We get all wet and everything, but we soon dry out. I've been caught in the rain riding my horse many times. I got all wet. My horse got all wet. But then I went to the trees and got protection. Go under a tree, you don't get that wet. The sunshine gets pretty hot sometimes, but there's a reason for that also. Without sunshine, none of these things would live.

Have kindness to all the living things. Not just the animals. I mean the plants and trees, and the grass—all have life. When I was younger I used to like to shoot things. Especially when I got my first gun. My grand-aunt, who was a medicine woman, gave me this teaching. We were walking one time and we came upon a rattlesnake. I got scared. I started to pick up a rock and she stopped my hand. She went over and broke off a willow switch about three feet long and left some leaves on the end of it. She took that switch and chased the snake away.

"Let him live. He belongs on this land like we do. He was made by the Creator just like we were."

This gave me a lot of thought, because many times I've come across rattlesnakes. A long time ago I used to kill snakes, but I don't do that anymore. Now, in later life, I realize I was destroying some of the Creator's creations. I always think of my grandaunt. Little teachings like that along the way give you a lot of thought.

I'm a provider in my family and part of that has to do with hunting. Once I was out hunting and chased an elk over the hill. I just seen it go over, so I went up, way up there and over the hill. When I got over to the other side, the fog really set in quick. It was so foggy I could hardly see the trees. I started going and I just felt I was going the wrong way. I stopped and I could see a big tree with a lot of branches out. So I got underneath and it was dry there. I sat there and smoked a cigarette. That's when I used to smoke. I kind of thought in my mind, "Which way am I going to go?" So I made up my mind, "I'm going to go this way." I started going and made my way through the fog.

It reminds me of a four-way stop. The four directions is the way I look at it. You come to the four directions and you're not supposed to wait there too long. You got to make a decision about which way you're going to go. Don't stand there and look around. You're supposed to know which way you're going. The old people tell me, when you get lost, you stand there and look around and try to find out which way you're supposed to go. Don't start panicking and run this way or that way.

I take my time and make sure that if I do go the wrong way I'll say, "Well, it's my fault." Sometimes you get off the track, get lost, lose direction. You got to have time to think something over to do it. You get in a hurry and sometimes you don't do the right thing. I've always been taught that.

Same way when you make something. When you're working on something, you try not to get finished too fast. You're going along there and you get in a hurry and then you get quite a ways ahead. You think you're ahead and then you look back. You got one place where you made a mistake. You have to take all that off and start over again. I was always taught perfection. That's one of my teachings that I always carry. My grandpa used to tell me, "Whatever you do, do it right. If I go out and hang one on, I do it the best I can!"

So you got to connect all these things. You got to use your head. You got to remember. Everything is put there for us to use. The Creator made us strong people. He gave us the ability to learn and to do things. The old people in my life didn't know how to read or write, but they still had a mind. It was given by the Creator to decide things, how to do things. How to use their talents, knowledge, how to express their thoughts. I lived a part of that life and I still look back to it for direction of my inner feelings, because they're the strongest things that taught me. What the Creator gave to all my people is in their hearts and in mine. That's where I get my direction—from their hearts.

I've used these abilities in my life, like how to make things out of animal skins or out of wood. I use my abilities to dance, sing, have fun, enjoy life. I even sit back and root for my favorite teams. I enjoy everything that needs to be enjoyed. You've got to use what the Creator gave you. This is a teaching that I've gained in my life that I'd like people to understand: you've got to use your abilities. He gave us a mind to use in any situation. You have to use your mind to decide what you want to do. The time I was in prison had to be a teaching from my own wrongdoing. It made a spot where I had a long time to think about a lot of these things.

I think about where I sit now: the family that I have, my children, this woman that made me a very happy man. I have no regrets about this life. Many things have happened along the line that were not right, but I guess it's what we call the teasing that I got along the way. I was able to withstand all these teasing things. Now I'm here and I do the best I can with everything and everybody. I know I'm always subject to criticism, but I can withstand this because I was taught this is teasing. "This is teasing you." I hope all my younger people don't get teased to the point where they become angry and make the wrong decisions. I hope I can, in some way, from my heart, give someone else direction.

Most of us stress education to our young people, and they forget to ask for wisdom from an elder such as a grandmother, uncle, aunt, or grandpa. People are forgetting to do this. I've gotten a lot of advice from my elders, especially the ones who couldn't read, write, or speak English.

I've also learned a lot of these things by, I guess you call it, the hard way. Maybe I've also punished myself a little bit to realize there is a good way. By these things, I keep it strong in my heart that I will reflect some of these good things that I've done for the young people, my family members, my children, grandchildren, and great-grandchildren. Maybe some day, great-great-grandchildren or even further. I've enjoyed life. I've enjoyed the many, many people I've come in contact with. In our Long House way we say, "I think I've touched a lot of people."

Epilogue

There's something about Horace that I can't quite put my finger on. Most of the time he's a regular guy. He likes to watch TV, travel, and take a nap when he's tired. Then there are the times when his presence attracts animals in an unusual way. He attacts eagles to him. They spiral high above him in wide circles. I have seen it happen more than a few times.

There is the relaxed side of Horace when he wears comfortable running shoes and laughs at jokes, his own or someone else's. And there are the times Horace comforts grieving families when a relative has passed on to "The Good Land." I have seen him in all these roles, yet I can't say I understand him completely. To be around Horace is like stepping into a place where time and space are meaningless words. The past becomes the present and the future unrolls before your eyes. It is quite possible he is not aware of his ability to make people focus on the moment, to bend time as if it were a piece of thin plastic. He is a puzzle, this friend of mine.

Once in a while someone appears, seemingly out of nowhere, and you find yourself listening, really listening, to what he says and the way he says it. That person may not even be talking to you, yet you hear his words as if they were meant especially for your ears. His words may direct your thoughts to your connection to the rest of the people on the planet, every living thing, the natural elements, all that you see, hear, taste, touch, and sense. For a brief time, maybe for just a moment, you'll feel the connection and believe it's possible to be human and still be a part of everything around you.

In this country we are familiar with religious leaders. They usually appear on television with heavy makeup on their rapturous faces and cheer us on to pray, pray, pray. But what do we know about spiritual leaders? Who are these quiet people who act every bit as human as the rest of us, yet emanate love and compassion without ever saying a word? Some of these people have followings, but many do not. Most of them do not want you to trail after them, imitating their every move. If, someday, you do find yourself next to a spiritual leader, all you really have to do is listen. Listen with your soul and the rest will take care of itself.

Glossary

The Nez Perce people (*Nimíipu*) have had a rich oral tradition
for at least ten thousand years. While it is true they did not
have a written language, that, in no way, diminishes their
sophisticated and poetic form of communication.
Approximately thirty years ago, linguist Haruo Aoki began
work on the Nez Perce Dictionary. His dictionary, now used
as a resource in the Nez Perce language classes that Horace
teaches at Lewis-Clark State College, is the guide I have used
to spell and translate the words in this memoir. Both Horace
and I would like to point out, however, that there are a variety
of ways to spell Nez Perce words, and no one style has been
formally adopted by the Nez Perce Tribe as of this writing.

Aoki writes, "There are many more languages in the world
than there are writing systems. The result is that most languages do not have a writing system tailor-made for them."

This is true for the Nez Perce language. For instance, the
letter "c" is pronounced as a hard "ts" sound. The letter "q" is
pronounced from farther back in the throat, as is the letter "x." I
have attempted to give you an approximation of sound by provid-
ing a phonetic spelling following the Nez Perce word. For a more

complete understanding of pronounciation and the ways in which the Nez Perce language is different from English, please refer to *The Nez Perce Dictionary* by Haruo Aoki, University of California Press.

M.A.

---

halxpaawinaq'it (hallh-pow-eet-NAH-kit). Translated as Monday. Literally means "completing Sunday."

halxpaawit (hallh-POW-eet). Translated as Sunday. Literally means "Sabbath rest or Sabbath."

halxpawit'asx (hallh-pow-ee-TAHSK). Translated as Saturday. Literally means "toward Sundaying."

hamtic' (HAM-tits). Hurry up.

'ipetes (ih-PEH-tes). Feather.

Long House. A building used for Seven Drum religious services and ceremonies.

Long House People. The people who practice the Seven Drum Religion at a Long House.

Lookingglass. Also spelled Looking Glass. He was a Nez Perce chief during the 1877 war.

miyooxat (mee-YOH-hot). A leader, a religious leader.

Nimiipu (ni-MEE-poo). Literally means "The People."

Nimiipuutimpt (ni-mee-poo-TIMPT). The Nez Perce Language. Literally means "The People's language."

Old Chief Joseph. The father of Chief Joseph.

pilaqa' (pi-LAH-ka). Maternal grandfather.

qalaca' (ka-LAH-tsa). Maternal grandfather.

qiwn (keewn). The Old Man. He is the entity that looks over the sweat house and the people who sweat within the sweat house.

Seven Drum Religion. The English name for Nez Perce Indian religion. Known in *Nimiipuutimpt* as *ipnuncilipt* (ip-NOON-see-lilpt) or *walahsat* (wah-LAH-saht). Seven drummers are usually asked to sing for ceremonies.

The Good Land, The Good Place. The final resting place for the spirits of the deceased, where all the Indian people go to reunite with their families and friends. The Seven Drum Religion does not include a version of "Hell," the way Christianity does. When the missionaries tried to explain Hell to the Nez Perce people, the closest translation they could come to was a description of a dump. This dumping ground of souls became the early Christian Nez Perces understanding of Hell.

weyekin (WAY-ya-kin). The power bestowed to a person by an animal or other being of nature.

White Bird. A Nez Perce chief, and headman of the Salmon River band, during the 1877 war.

wistitamo (wis-tih-TAH-mo). A sweat house.

A LITTLE BIT OF WISDOM

was designed by Caroline Hagen and set in
Cochin — a French-inspired typeface developed in the
nineteenth century and renowed for its clarity and
accessible style — on a Macintosh 8100.
This book is printed on acid-free paper by
Data Reproductions.